The Ultimate Blackjack System To Riches

DarkStar with Paul Martin

For comments or feedback, Contact Us at: welovemail@darkstarblackjack.com

Cover Design: Robin Krupnow

Limit of Liability / Disclaimer of Warranty:

While the publisher and author have used their best efforts in preparing this book, they make no representations or warranties regarding the accuracy or completeness of the contents of this book. The publisher and author specifically disclaim any implied warranties of merchantability or fitness for a particular purpose, and make no guarantees whatsoever that you will achieve any particular result. Any case studies that are presented herein do not necessarily represent what you should expect to achieve, since business success depends on a variety of factors. We believe all case studies and results presented herein are true and accurate, but we have not audited the results. The advice and strategies contained in this book may not even be suitable for your situation, and you should consult your own advisors as appropriate. The publisher and the author shall not be held liable for any loss of profit or any other commercial damages, including but not limited to special, incidental, consequential, or other damages. The fact that an organization or website is referred to in this work as a citation and/ or a potential source of information does not mean that the publisher or author endorses the information the organization or website may provide or the recommendations it may make. Further, readers should be aware that Internet websites listed in this work may have changed or disappeared after this work was written.

Earnings Disclaimer: We don't believe in get rich programs— all human progress and accomplishment takes hard work. As stipulated by law, we cannot and do not make any guarantees about your ability to get results or earn any money with our ideas, information, tools or strategies. After all, it takes hard work to succeed in any type of business. In fact, it takes hard work to succeed at ANYTHING in life— try learning to play the guitar without putting in any work, and see how that goes! Your results in life are up to you and the amount of effort and resources that you are willing to put into succeeding. Nothing in this book or any of our websites is a promise or guarantee of results or future earnings, and we do not offer any legal, medical, tax or other professional advice. Any financial numbers referenced here, or on any of our sites, are simply estimates or projections, and should not be considered exact, actual or as a promise of potential earnings— all numbers are illustrative only. In fact, the average person who purchases this book and other programs never finishes the book, never puts the work into implementing the strategies taught, and therefore achieves little to no results.

Introduction

My name is DarkStar. I am a Blackjack dealer for a big casino and I am a professional Blackjack player. I am writing this book to give Blackjack players all over the world something they have never had before--inside access to the top level, ultra-secret operations of casino security and gaming and the methods they employ to observe, detect and control Blackjack players like you. If my cover is blown, I will immediately be terminated as a casino employee, and I will be banned from playing professionally at all of the casinos that surround me. So I am the Dark Star surrounded by big casino lights.

For the longest time, I was a normal person, perhaps like you. I meandered from job to job making a living, sometimes with a good paycheck but often times just getting by. When I was clearing $100k, my stress level was off the charts. I was the bitch-slave manager of a major corporation. Yes, I lived in a nice house, ate at fancy restaurants and drove nice cars, but I was miserable. When I traded down jobs to acquire a more levelheaded and sane life, I was happier, but my paycheck was barely paying the bills, and I was spending more time at McDonald's and Walmart, than I was willing to admit. Don't get me wrong. I am not a high society snob, but I don't like to scratch around on the ground to make a living like a chicken does for its next meal. There had to be a better way.

Who wants to live from paycheck-to-paycheck, just getting by. Do you? I know I don't.

Maybe your situation was like mine. You go to work, do the long commute, exchange morning pleasantries with coworkers you would never associate with outside of work because you have nothing in common. You get along with your bosses but you really don't like them. You spend your day toiling away at boring tasks and sit in endless company meetings, listening to some flunkie middle manager with the intelligence of a Barbie Doll, drone on and on about some stupid new policy or procedure they just thought up, that they got permission from the idiots upstairs to roll out, all with the effect of making your company and even more miserable place to work at. The clock finally strikes 5 and you rush out the door for another long commute home, only to RINSE & REPEAT the whole process, day after day, week after week, month after month, with no possible end in sight.

I did this for years, sorry to say. What a waste of a life! The things we do to feed our families, pay the electric bills, and keep the creditors at bay. It can really be a hard life. But you have to be open and ready to react when a fresh opportunity presents itself; when a better path beats its way to your door. That happened to me when I met Enoch.

Enoch is not his real name, but his cover for this book. Like me, Enoch is a professional Blackjack player. Enoch and I met at work. You know one of those jobs I described earlier. Enoch paid his way through college playing Blackjack. I had heard about the MIT Blackjack team while I was in college but never met anyone who knew how to count cards. I was fascinated and asked him to tell me more about it.

I had tried more than once to start a business of my own and immediately had a thought. I asked Enoch, "What if I staked you and you played Blackjack with my money and we split the profits?" I don't trust people easily but if you got to know Enoch you'd see why I would trust him with my life savings if not my life. His answer will give you some insight into the kind of guy he is. He said, "Why would I do that when I can just teach you to do it yourself?" I was prepared to hand him ten thousand bucks and instead he wanted to give me free lessons so I could go out and make my own money.

I replied that there was no way I could count cards. He was far better at math than I and much more intelligent overall. While that is completely true, he still insisted I had the ability to learn card-counting and I agreed to give it a shot.

First we started with what I knew. He asked if I had played Blackjack and if I knew Basic Strategy. I said yes to both questions but when he quizzed me on Basic Strategy we learned I only knew the microwave version. I'll explain the microwave version later in the book. Memorizing Basic Strategy was easy enough but when it came time for the first card-counting lesson I almost threw in the towel. If this happens to you, remember riding a bike was not so easy the first time either. Would you have thought, as a child, that after a little practice you'd be able to balance that thing without even thinking about it. That it would be as natural as walking. Counting cards will get like that if you put in the time.

After months of practice Enoch and I hit the road for the casinos. We had some fun and made a little money. Looking back we were both clueless. After discovering it was not enough to live on, I said it was time to sharpen the ax and we put our playing on hold.

I started learning everything I could about card-counting and learned that the pros refer to it as advantaged play because it means you have the advantage rather than the house. Just because you know how to count cards does not mean you are an advantage player. You also need to know exactly how to use that information. Enoch and I were missing much of that key information. He was good enough to make a living in college with some help from his parents and we did not lose money but we were guessing on a lot of the finer details. I have read dozens of books on Blackjack, taken online trainings and participated in blogs and chat rooms with some of the best Blackjack players in the world. In fact, not long after I started really studying the game, Enoch commented that the student had become the master.

Why Blackjack?

Blackjack is unique to all other casino games in that the player can actually gain the advantage over the house. It is important that you understand that this only applies to Blackjack. The other game in the casino where people can make a living is Poker but that is because you are not playing against the house. Carnival games like Ultimate Texas Hold-EM where you do play against the house are not beatable in the long run. If you win playing one of these games it is due to luck. The reason Blackjack is different is that current events affect future events. This is called random dependent events. Since once a card is dealt out of the shoe or deck it cannot be dealt again until the next shoe, it is possible to predict the outcome of the next round. Games like Roulette and Craps are games that involve random independent events. The roulette ball or dice do not have memory but cards in Blackjack do. If a seven comes up in craps, there is no reason why it cannot come up again. But if you play single deck Blackjack and four Aces come out in the first round, there is no way you will see another Ace til the dealer shuffles. This is true for Baccarat as well but that game is structured in a way that makes counting useless. Card counting tells you the cards remaining but not the order they are in. You would need to know the order the cards are in to correctly predict a Banker or Player win in Baccarat.

Why Read This Book?

1) Because this is the best book on Blackjack ever written. I know because I have read most of the other books out there. Some of them are good and I cite these later in the book, but most of them are inadequate, at best, filled with misinformation that will set you on a disastrous path. Because I have read all of the major Blackjack publications-- books, e books, websites and blogs—I have separated the wheat from the chaff. I will keep you from stepping in the manure and help you find the pearls.

2) You want to make a good living playing Blackjack. You're sick of working for the man and want to be your own boss, set your own schedule, work the days you want to work, and do it in an exciting and lively atmosphere. In this book, you will find everything you need to become a competent and professional Blackjack player. Almost everything I teach you is based on mathematical proofs, not on opinions or myths. You will benefit from the thousands and thousands of hours I have spent in casinos testing and perfecting almost every possible play, every procedure, every turn of the card.

I will teach you about when to load-up the bet and when to get the hell out of the casino. I know all the pitfalls to avoid, when the house is getting wise to you. I have tested my playing and betting scenarios literally into the billions of trials using sophisticated software, so when I tell you something works, I have quantifiable proof to back it up.

3) I have all of the inside information. I work on both sides of the table. I know when the house is watching you. I am keeping the count right along with you. I know your next move before you do. I know and recognize all the mistakes that card counters make, even good ones who think they are fooling me. I can spot them a mile away. I know what security (the eye-in-the-sky) is looking for. I can teach you how to camouflage your card counting and betting. I can teach you how to look like an ordinary chump casino player that casino management likes, instead of a lethal professional that they have their radar antennas scanning the tables for. I know the mistakes and poor assumptions that casino security and casino management makes. Working on the inside has made me privy to all of their weaknesses and has raised my game to the next level. I can do the same for you.

4) I have risked my own money as proof. Let's face it, in casino gaming, the

proof is in the risk and reward. I have made a living out of winning Blackjack, and I have lost more than my share of Blackjack games. I will tell you from the outset that in Blackjack, even when you are in your best form at the top of your game, playing the best possible strategy with the most accurate information available to you...you will lose more hands than you will win. That is a fact that you need to embrace now. The good news is, that you can make more money than you lose, just by how you play the game. I will teach you how.

5) I make no claims that I can't back up. A lot of Blackjack books will promise you untold wealth. I don't make any such promises. I stick to the facts. I will teach you how, in the long run, you will make more money than you will lose. I will leave the Limousines, the Cristal Champagne, and life of luxury tales to other fictional Blackjack books. I run my Blackjack business like a tight ship that would make a Wall Street Hedge Fund firm proud. I keep track of every penny, every expense, every gas receipt, and every dealer tip. This is not a book about wearing the biggest diamond rings and being the loudmouth at the tables. It's about flying under the radar and playing Blackjack like a Ninja making a good living and sleeping well at night.

6) Hear some amazing stories. This is one of the biggest motivators for me to write this book. As a dealer, and more so as a professional Blackjack player have both heard and witnessed some amazing things. I have kept a detailed journal along the way and I hope that you too will laugh and be equally amazed at more than a decade spent in the casinos.

Why Am I Writing This Book?

Give a man a fish and you feed him for a day; teach a man to fish and you feed him for a lifetime. I am writing for several reasons, but the biggest is to help you. I believe in giving back to society. When she treats you right you owe a debt to your fellow man to help him prosper. I am making no promises of riches. This is not a stupid Bernie Madoff get-rich pyramid scheme. This is not a send me money now, and I'll tell you how, book. This is not a book filled with empty platitudes and baseless concoctions for achieving wealth. This is a real book, filled with scientific proofs and sound mathematical structure.

It's not just bad Blackjack books that are contaminating our society. Money management and Investment books proclaim the "GET RICH QUICK" mantra all the time. It is my opinion that books like: Think & Grow Rich…How To Make Millions by…The 4-Hour Work Week…How to Get Filthy Rich…Get Rich Quick, The Road to Wealth…though they may be entertaining to read, are a dead-end to nowhere.

You can't get rich just because someone tells you so. Look at all the famous Rich people. Warren Buffet built his wealth slowly over a lifetime. Bill Gates started a company at the right place at the right time. Oprah Winfrey. It didn't happen fast for her. She worked damn hard over decades to build her wealth.

This is an investment book. Before I played Blackjack professionally I traded stocks and options. Once I learned card-counting or advantage play as it is more accurately referred to I gave up gambling on Wall Street. Not because I could make more money playing Blackjack but because it was less risky. Blackjack is predictable. No matter what happens in the world there are going to be 52 cards in that deck and the rules of the game will not change in the middle of the shoe. The same cannot be said for Wall Street.

Jim Cramer, a famous hedge fund manager who now has a show on CNBC called Mad Money, also happens to be a very good Blackjack player. In an interview with Tim Russert the topic of Blackjack came up. While Mr. Cramer prefers the stock market and I prefer Blackjack, I think his comments on Blackjack are insightful and actually support my argument in favor of Blackjack. Here is an excerpt from the transcript taken from NBCNEWS.com:

CRAMER: The important thing is, never take a drink. They want you to drink so badly. You—just ask for that bottle of water. Constantly ask for the water. Never take anything else.

RUSSERT: Is there a higher rate of return from the blackjack table or the stock market?

CRAMER: Oh, the stock market's much easier. The stock market is much—though I've got to tell you, Blackjack is fair. I've never seen anyone rig blackjack.

RUSSERT: And you've seen someone rig the market?

CRAMER: Oh, all the time.

RUSSERT: Give me a name.

CRAMER: Well, look, Enron rigged it. WorldComm rigged it. We see rigging fairly regularly. [1]

I am going to teach you how to fish. The question is, are you willing to put in the time and effort? This is a hard road. Not everybody gets to be a Navy Seal or a Harvard Lawyer. You have to work hard -- really hard. You're going to spend long hours in casinos. Most of them will be filled with cigarette smoke and your eyes will burn after hours and hours of playing. You will be forced to listen to inane stories and mythical Blackjack sermons delivered from the pulpits of the casinos, by countless potato-head players who claim to be experts at their craft but are dim witted dunces throwing away their money. You will go back again and again. A lot of dealers will recognize you and know your name. The casino is your office. You will spend so much time here and so much time playing that you will master the game and practically play in your sleep.

Finally, I am writing this to dispel the progressive betting myth. If you read nothing else, please read that chapter. Too many people are losing more money than they should because of books on progressive betting. This book is primarily written for people who want to pursue an alternative source of income but even the recreational player will benefit from the chapter on progressive betting.

The Promise Land

If you do stick it out, you will reap the benefits of being your own boss. Never again answering to anyone else. Setting your own schedule. Taking days off when you want them. Your workplace can vary from Reno to Las Vegas to Atlantic City to the Bahamas or Puerto Rico. There are countless places you have to practice your profession. Best of all, you will be working for yourself. You will meet some fascinating people, here some amazing stories. You will do things your way, and hopefully like me, have some fun along the way.

1. http://www.nbcnews.com/id/22297081/ns/msnbc-the_ed_show/t/tim-russert-dec/#.VVwfLflVlko

♡ Chapter 1 – The Game of Blackjack

If you are certain that you know the rules of Blackjack and how they vary from casino to casino you can skip this chapter. If you think you know the rules but believe that all casinos have the same rules on Blackjack you need to read this chapter.

A Short History Lesson

Blackjack is one of the oldest card games in the world and the most popular table game in the casino. I doubt you could find more than one adult who has never heard of Blackjack but I would bet you could not find more than one who knows why it is called Blackjack.

Originally Blackjack was simply called 21, and if you were dealt a ten value card and an Ace as your first 2 cards, it was called a natural and you would be paid a bonus if the dealer did not also have a natural. The bonus was 3 to 2 or 1.5 times your bet. When Nevada casinos introduced the game, they decided to spice it up by paying a larger bonus for an Ace and a Jack of Spades or Clubs (i.e. a Black Jack) dealt on the first 2 cards. The bonus for this enhanced Blackjack was as high as 10:1 in some casinos.

All of this transpired before Edward Thorp's book, Beat The Dealer, which introduced basic strategy and a very simple count system. That book was very popular, and while most people who read it did not learn to count, they did learn to play much smarter. As a result, the casinos realized a player armed with basic strategy who received a bonus larger than 3:2 for any kind of Blackjack would actually have an advantage over the house. In fact, at one time, you could find small casinos in Nevada that offered single-deck Blackjack with rules so favorable to the player that it was possible to gain a very slight advantage over the house without counting cards and with just a 3:2 standard Blackjack payout. Today the casino only has a 0.75% advantage over a player using basic strategy in a regular Blackjack game with Las Vegas Strip rules. That is ¾ of one percent! We will never see a bonus like that again. In fact, it is becoming increasingly difficult to get a payoff of 3 to 2. Most casinos on the Vegas strip now pay 6 to 5 for a natural. I was in Vegas when 6 to 5 was first introduced and the casinos actually put up large signs that advertised 6 to 5 on Blackjack. I think they thought people may be stupid or drunk enough to focus on the 6 and think that's twice as good as 3 to 2. I think they were probably right, at least for some people.

Rules

1. Blackjack may be played with one to eight decks of 52-card decks.

2. Aces may be counted as 1 or 11 points, 2 thru 9 according to pip value, and tens and face cards count as ten points.

3. The value of a hand is the sum of the point values of the individual cards. Except, a "Blackjack" is the highest hand, consisting of an ace and any 10-point card delivered as the first 2 cards, and it outranks all other 21-point hands. If you split aces and receive a 10-point card, it is not Blackjack.

4. After the players have bet, the dealer will give two cards to each player and two cards to himself. One of the dealer cards is dealt face up. The face down card is called the "hole card."

5. If the dealer has an ace showing, he will offer a side bet called "insurance." This side wager pays 2 to 1 if the dealer's hole card is any 10-point card. Insurance wagers are optional and may not exceed half the original wager. Players with a Blackjack are offered "even money" which is essentially the same as "insurance". If the player accepts even money she will win the amount of the bet immediately before the dealer checks his hole card.

6.   If the dealer has a ten or an ace showing (after offering insurance with an ace showing), then he will peek at his face down card to see if he has a Blackjack. If he does, then he will turn it over immediately.

7.   If the dealer does have a Blackjack, then all wagers (except insurance) will lose, unless the player also has a Blackjack, which will result in a push. The dealer will resolve insurance wagers at this time.

8.   Play begins with the player to the dealer's left. The following are the choices available to the player:

- Stand: Player stands pat with his cards.

- Hit: Player draws another card (and more if he wishes). If this card causes the player's total points to exceed 21 (known as "breaking" or "busting") then he loses.

- Double Down: Player doubles his bet and gets one, and only one, more card.

- Split: If the player has a pair, or any two 10-point cards, then he may double his bet and separate his cards into two individual hands. The dealer will automatically give each card a second card. The player may hit, stand, or double normally.

- The rules on splitting vary depending on the casino

1.   DAS – Double-after-split allowed means that the player may double -down and get one additional card only just like the Double-down option above. This is never offered when splitting

Aces

2. Re-split and Re-split Aces
– In some casinos you can
split again if you get
another card of equal
value after splitting. You
will be allowed to split to
3 or 4 hands if this option
is offered. It may be
offered on anything other
than Ace Splits. Even if
Re-splitting of Aces is
allowed the player will be
given only one additional
card for each Ace unless
it is another Ace.

• Surrender: The player forfeits half his wager,
keeping the other half, and does not play out
his hand. This option is only available on the
initial two cards, and depending on casino
rules, sometimes it is not allowed at all.

9. After each player has had his turn, the dealer will turn
over his hole card. If the dealer has 16 or less, then he
will draw another card. A special situation is when the
dealer has an ace and any number of cards totaling six
points (known as a "soft 17"). At some tables, the
dealer will also hit a soft 17.

10. If the dealer goes over 21 points, then any player who
didn't already bust will win.

11. If the dealer does not bust, then the higher point total
between the player and dealer will win.

12. Winning wagers pay even money, except a winning
player Blackjack usually pays 3 to 2.

- Some casinos have been short-paying Blackjacks, which is a rule strongly in the casino's favor.

Gambling Etiquette

For those who have never played a table game before, this section is for you.

- Understand the rules before you sit down. Even better, understand the rules before you walk in the casino.

- Buy chips from the dealer (Buy-in) or cash in chips (Cash-out) between hands only. If you sit down while a hand is in progress, wait patiently for the conclusion of the hand before you buy-in. Use this time to get your money ready.

- Know that RED CHIPS are $5, GREEN CHIPS are $25, and BLACK CHIPS are $100.

- At the table you may ask the dealer to make change for a large denomination chip.

- When you cash out, the dealers prefer for you to trade in smaller denominations of chips rather than larger ones. Between playing hands, give the dealer neat stacks of chips and let him/her count them and change them in.

- In some games the cards are dealt face up. If this is the case, never touch your cards. If the cards are dealt face down, then touch your cards with one hand only! If you break this rule, you will almost always get a sharp rebuke. Be gentle with the cards; don't bend them or put drinks on them. Some players have tried to cheat by bending specific cards slightly, for example the aces, and the dealers have to guard against this.

- Never touch your bet once the first card has been dealt. Wait until after the hand is over.

- Verbal instructions are not enough. You must use hand signals so that the eye-in-the-sky camera positioned above the table, can view your intent.

Blackjack Hand Signals

Cards are dealt face up:

Hit: Tap the table with your finger.

Stand: Wave your hand, palm open and down, parallel to the table.

Double-Down/Split: Place your matching bet next to your original bet, but never on top of your original bet. If you are doubling down, simply place your matching bet next to the original bet. If you have a matching pair and you would like to split the cards, hold out two fingers in the shape of a "V." The dealer may choose to adjust your betting stacks according to casino house protocol.

Bust: If the total of your cards exceeds 21, in other words you bust, then do nothing and the dealer will immediately collect your cards and place them in the discard tray.

Cards are dealt face down:

Hit: Lightly brush or scrape the cards against the felt of the table, or tap on top of your cards or next to the cards if they are lying face down.

Stand: Slide your cards face down under or directly next to your bet. Do not lift your chips in the process. This is known as tucking your cards and is sometimes a difficult skill to learn. Simply try to slide your cards face down under your bet without touching your bet with your hand.

Double-down/Split: Place your cards face up on the

table, just above your bet. Place your matching bet next to your original bet, but never on top of your original bet. If you are doubling down, simply place your matching bet next to the original bet. If you have a matching pair and you would like to split the cards, hold out two fingers in the shape of a "V." The dealer may chose to adjust your betting stacks according to casino house protocol.

Bust: If the total of your cards exceeds 21, in other words you bust, then lay down your cards face up next to your bet.

Blackjack: As already described a Blackjack is any ten-valued card and any Ace delivered as the first two cards. If you get this in a hand-held game simply lay them down face up in front of your bet. You can do this at any time. You do not need to wait your turn.

♣ Chapter 2 - Blackjack Myths

If you think there's a pattern or an exploitable rhythm to this game, if you think there are biases or dumping tables, or predictable hot or cold dealers, you better save your Blackjack playing for Disneyworld. For as sure as twenty beats a twelve, you're playing in Fantasyland. Attention TARGET players. It's not too late to play this game properly. --Don Schlesinger/Blackjack Attack

"Do you know what the difference between praying in church and praying in the casino is? In the casino you mean it." –Ken Uston

There are a lot of myths about gambling in general, and Blackjack specifically. I'd like to take the time to address them here in order for you to become familiar with them, so that you don't fall into the trap so very many players do. If you want to play Blackjack like a professional, you have to give up on these silly superstitions.

Of course the biggest myth of all is the streak myth which leads to progressive betting. I cover that one in a separate chapter because it is the most prevalent and dangerous. If you do not already play much Blackjack the rest of these may sound silly but you'll be surprised how many people believe them.

Martingale Betting System

If winning streaks are a myth then what about a reverse progression? That must be what Martingale was thinking.

Along with Fries, we can thank the French for this beauty. Martingale says that you should double your bet every time you lose until you eventually win. The premise being you can't lose forever. If the table limit AND your bankroll were both equal to infinity, this would actually work. It's an example of how theory and reality can be completely opposed.

Just for fun, let's look at the math in a possible example:

Losses
$5+$10+$20+$40+$80+$160+$320+$640+$1280+$2560+$5120+$10240+$20480+$40960+$81920 = 163,835

$81,920 x 2 = 163,840 (your next bet)

Then you bet 163,840 and WIN!

Drum-roll as we do the math...163,840 - 163,835 = $5 net profit.

In fact, no matter how many times you repeat this reverse progression, if you eventually win the last bet, your profit will be exactly equal to your initial bet.

It is possible to lose every single hand. One time, I lost every single hand on a 6-deck shoe. Think about that. That's twenty-something hands in a row that I lost! Way more than the betting schedule shown above. So don't even think about employing this method.

The Table That Plays "Right" Will Win

Another myth that is specific to Blackjack, is that everyone should play "right." Apparently "right" indicates that players play according to the guidelines of Basic Strategy. If everyone at the table plays "right," then everyone at the table will win. This particular piece of dogma implies that Blackjack has suddenly become a team-sport.

Stop to think about this. If you and I are sitting at the same table, and I lose my money but I was playing according to Basic Strategy, you are not likely to reimburse me if you won. Let's carry this fallacy a little further for the sake of amusement and logic. If playing "right" was a valid Blackjack strategy, then if all players seated at a table had Basic Strategy instruction cards in front of them and played strictly in accordance with Basic Strategy, then the house would lose every time. A group of people could walk into a casino and break the bank by simply playing Basic Strategy and the casino would go out of business.

I don't understand how anyone could possibly believe this is true. Yet the people that believe in this fruit loop theory believe there's some kind of underlying logic or math to support this nonsense. These players really believe that the cards will come out in a certain correct order and we will all win as long as we all play "right." But the moment somebody deviates from playing "right," they somehow change the cards, and "that's why we're losing."

I once played at a table next to a guy betting $100 per hand or more at a $5 minimum table. Anyone willing to bet $100 a hand would have their choice of at least 30 tables in this joint.

After losing several hands in a row he stood up, slammed his fist on the table and shouted, "I've had enough! I lost three grand since that bitch sat down at the table!"

He was referring to an older lady that sat down at least 45 minutes ago and was mostly guessing at how to play her hand, rather than abiding by any particular strategy. I could hardly believe someone would lash out at a perfect stranger, much less a grandma.

I said, in her defense, "Yeah! I saw her reaching across the table and putting your chips in the betting circle! It most certainly was her fault!"

Not impressed with my sarcasm but having no immediate reply, he simply stormed off. The woman, to her credit, simply sat quiet and continued to play as she wished.

This belief is not limited to people who know Basic Strategy. You would think that if you believe everyone at the table must play "right" or "by the book" as they often say, then they would know and play according to the Basic Strategy chart themselves. This is rarely the case. First of all most people

who claim to play "by the book" have never read a single book on Blackjack. Furthermore, they don't even know Basic Strategy or if they do know it, they choose to ignore some of the recommendations.

Third Base Controls the Outcome

I once sat down at third base in the middle of a shoe with a high positive count. Third base is the seat furthest to the dealer's right and the last player to act on his or her hand.

The lady playing next to me said, "If you are going to sit there, then you better know how to play!"

Slightly astonished by her rudeness to a complete stranger, I replied that I hadn't a clue.

Basic Strategy states that you should hit until you have 17 or better if the dealer's "up card" is a 7 or better. On the very first hand after she made this statement the dealer displayed a 7 as his "up card" and this lady had a Ten and a Four or 14. After finishing her conversation with the man standing behind her she waived her hand indicating "stand". You may not know it yet, but this is not even close to the right play. I had 16, hit, and received a 5 for a perfect 21. The dealer flipped a 10 under his 7 for 17. Most of the players won because this is the lowest total that the dealer is allowed to stand on.

When I asked her why she stood on a 14 after telling me I better play right, she replied, "That's why I don't play third base."

I had no response. I almost told her that with no one sitting at physical third base, she was the effective third base, being last to act on her hand but thought better of it.

I remembered a Dilbert cartoon I once had in my office that stated, "Never argue with an idiot. They drag you down to their level then beat you with experience."

This is close to the last myth except, in this case, only the last player to act must do so with care. In the case described above, it apparently matters what exact chair you use, but most of the faithful believe it's the last player to act that controls the outcome of the game. The fun comes when third base plays "wrong" and everyone wins anyhow. This will not shake their faith in the slightest.

Instead they will say, "we may have survived that one but we'll pay for it later."

The next loss will then be attributed to that bad behavior on the part of third base six rounds ago. The god of Blackjack shall have her revenge eventually and it will reign down upon the entire table like an Egyptian plague.

The Casino Cheats/The Shuffle Machine Cheats

Many Blackjack players want to see a hand shuffle because they think the machine is somehow slotting the cards in the house's favor. There are so many things wrong with this, that I don't know where to start.

How would the casino know how many people are going to play, whether and how many people are going to come into the table, when and whether people will leave the table, how people will play?

The casino has no reason to cheat. The house will win about 1% more than it loses in the long run even to people playing perfect Basic Strategy. Only a very skilled card counter can beat the house in the long run. The casino could easily lose their gaming license if caught cheating. That risk is not worth an extra advantage. If they want more profits on the game, all they have to do is add side bets with a tremendous house edge. In fact, that is exactly what they do.

Many professional players will advise against playing in Native American casinos because they are self-governed. This is not exactly true. There is a tribal gaming commission tasked with making sure the house runs a clean game. However the state and federal government also have inspectors to keep the casino honest.

The one place where there is no gaming commission at all is on a cruise ship. In fact, it is unclear what laws would even govern gaming on the high seas. Ships wait until they are in international water to open the casino. Even in this case, cheating by the house is not worth it. Dealers on cruise ships have Facebook accounts and may not work on the ship forever. Word would easily get out if a cruise line was cheating in their casino and the company would stand to lose more than just the gaming revenue. In fact, cruise ship casinos are actually more likely to side with the guest in any gaming dispute rather than risk the bad review.

Someone Must Be The Fall Guy

Another myth is, that if you have a full table of people playing at the table, somebody at the table has to take a hit or else the dealer won't bust.

Let's use the example that the dealer has a small card facing up, we'll say it's a 6. Basic Strategy will tell you that you should stand on your hand if you have 12 or higher, because you might bust, and you want to let the dealer bust. But, if you have 5 or 6 players at the table, a lot of people believe whoever has the lowest hand, we'll say it's you with a 12, should hit, because if you don't, the dealer is going to make a hand.

This is obviously just total superstition. Suppose you were alone at that table. Are you still supposed to hit your 12 against the dealers 6? Of course not! It makes no sense. Yet even when these fruit-loops are proved wrong, when no one hits and the dealer busts anyway, or someone hits and the dealer still doesn't bust, then they just assign this to the exception that proves the rule. However, if they actually kept track of this, they would find out there are more exceptions than rules.

The take away here is, whatever crazy theory people have, whenever they see a random example that proves their theory, they file that away as proof to be remembered. But every time they see an example that disproves their theory, they will conveniently forget that. Most players have selective memory—the ability to remember some facts while apparently forgetting others, especially when they are inconvenient or embarrassing.

Jumping Into the Middle of the Shoe/Coming Into the Table Late

Well this myth says, when a player comes to the table before the shoe has been completely dealt, and sits down to play a hand, this somehow causes the dealer to hit a Blackjack. And if it's not the dealer that hits a Blackjack, then it's always somebody else. Jumping into the middle of the shoe causes someone other than the fruit loop, to get Blackjack.

I once had a dealer tell me that this anomaly was true. She said, "Every time someone jumps in, I get Blackjack."

I was flabbergasted and I said to her, "Every time?"

So then she moderated her stance and said, "Well almost every time. Like 90%."

I said, "OK. Do you ever get Blackjack when no one jumps in?"

She says, "Of course!"

I said, "Well how the hell did that happen?"

The only way I can explain why all of these people believe in these crazy myths is, people think there has to be a reason for everything. Random occurrence is not acceptable. Why can we not accept that the cards are sitting in the shoe in random order and there is no reason why the cards came out in the order that they did? If you flip a coin, is there a reason it came up heads? It obviously cannot come up tails every time, despite the saying, "tails never fails".

Sitting out a Hand to Change the Cards

If a player has had a number of bad hands, sometimes you will see him sit out a hand to "change the cards."

Add a Hand to Change the Cards

Again, if a player is struggling with bad hands, and she wants to change the cards on purpose, she will add a hand, meaning she will play two hands instead of one.

Now what's beautiful about this from the casino's perspective is, most casinos will force you to bet double if you want to play two hands instead of one. So if the table minimum is $10, and you want to bet 2 hands, you will have to bet a minimum of $20 on each hand.

Think about that. You've been losing, say, 6 hands in a row, so the fruit loop theory is to quadruple your risk. Instead of betting $10, you should now bet $40, that's $20 on each hand, and that will fix the cards and you will start winning now.

Fifty-Dollar Bills are Bad Luck

It's not just in Blackjack. My dad played a lot of Craps, and if someone dropped a fifty-dollar bill on the table, he would immediately say, "I'm done," and he'd cash out and leave the table. If you see a fifty-dollar bill anywhere, that's like a black cat crossing your path.

I frequently throw fifty-dollar bills on the table because I want to get people off of the table right away. As a matter of fact, I will go to the casino with a stack of fifty-dollar bills, and buy into the table with $400, all in fifty-dollar bills, just to see if I can get some of the people to leave. It works really well.

The myth is so pervasive, in Vegas, for example, if you are cashing out $450 dollars, the cashier will usually ask you, "Is it OK if I give you a fifty?"

Chip Placement Orientation

Some people believe that you have to place the chip, particularly in a betting circle, in a certain orientation. So the image or icon on the chip has to be either facing the player, or facing the dealer, depending on whatever they believe. But if you have that chip twisted the wrong way, you are going to lose.

Black Eight Dealer Breaks

You will hear this from players and dealers alike. At this point I shouldn't have to explain how absurd this is.

Never Split Anything That Starts with an F

This is sometimes modified to, "Never split anything that starts with an F, Fours, Fives and Fucking Sixes." This is almost true. You never split Fives. You treat them as any other ten. Fours you split only against a dealer 5 or 6. Sixes can be split against any low card for the dealer (2-6).

Summary

I know that Blackjack isn't the only form of entertainment to have crazy superstitions. In theater they say, "Break a leg," before an actor takes the stage. In baseball it is taboo to mention that a particular pitcher might be about to pitch a perfect game, let alone think it! No, you can talk about the weather, your favorite TV show, what team you are playing tomorrow, the new pair of shoes you just bought, but definitely you must not say or be heard to say the words, "PERFECT GAME" or "PITCHING REALLY WELL." Hell, you might get beat up by your teammates!

♦ Chapter 3 - Basic Strategy and Game Selection

Basic Strategy was first published in the *Journal of the American Statistical Association , Vol. 51, 429-439* in 1956 by Roger Baldwin, Wilbert Cantley, Herbert Maisel and James McDermott titled "The Optimum Strategy in Blackjack". It was not widely known until Edward Thorp published it along with a detailed explanation of it in *Beat The Dealer* in 1962. Since that time it has been modified for the current game. In fact, Basic Strategy is slightly different depending on the rules for the Blackjack game you are playing.

On the next page is the Basic Strategy chart for the most common game found on the Las Vegas Strip. For simplicity, I am going to use the common abbreviations for the various rules. These rules will vary from casino to casino and even within the same casino depending on how many decks are being used and/or the minimum bet.

H17 – Dealer Hits Soft 17

S17 – Dealer Stands On All 17s

DAS – Double-after-split Allowed

NS – No Surrender

These are not the only rules that can vary but they are the only ones that affect Basic Strategy. Also, whenever I refer to a 10 or Ten I am talking about any card that has a value of 10 in the game of Blackjack. Tens, Jacks,

Queens and Kings are all 10s because it makes no difference which one you have. If your hand is Jack, King you have 20 same as King, King and both could be split. Many beginners think that only exact pairs can be split. This is not the case.

How to Choose a Game

The more options available to the player, the better. Also, it is much better if the dealer must stand on all 17's. It is also preferred to have as few decks as possible. It is a little complicated to evaluate games and determine which one is the most favorable for the professional player. At first glance, you might think the single-deck game is the best one. Until you realize that they only deal one hand and shuffle. You are not going to be able to gain much of an advantage counting in that game.

So you move on to Double-Deck Blackjack. This might be the best option, but choose wisely. Remember that more player options and dealer standing on ALL 17's is preferred. Many double-deck games will only allow you to double-down on ten or eleven, and no double-after-split.

Here is how the rules affect the house advantage in the six deck shoe game. The numbers are percentage points and a negative sign means that this rule reduces the house advantage or increases the player advantage. This assumes the player uses Basic Strategy and does not count. This was taken from "Blackjack Attack" by Don Schlesinger.[2]

Rule	Dealer Stands on All 17s	Dealer Hits Soft 17
Dealer Hits Soft 17	0.00	+0.215
No Double Downs	1.372	1.380
Double Any 1st 2 Cards	0	0
Double on 11 Only	0.633	0.639
Double on 10 or 11 Only	0.173	0.181
No Ace Split Allowed	0.180	0.180
Split Aces Once	0	0
Split Aces Twice to 3 Hands	-0.059	-0.059
Split Aces 3 Times to 4 Hands	-0.069	-0.068
No Splitting of Non-Ace Pairs	0.247	0.241
With Double-After-Split Allowed		
Split Non-Ace Pairs Only Once	-0.088	-0.091
Split Non-Ace Pairs Twice	-0.134	-0.0137
Split Non-Ace Pairs 3 Times	-0.142	-0.144

If you are not counting cards, the house always has the advantage. You can use this chart to evaluate the games you have the option of playing. Add up the values for all of the rules and then add the standard 0.546% advantage the house has for making its hand last. For example, you find a six deck shoe game where the dealer hits Soft 17, double-after-split is allowed, non-Aces can be split twice, Aces only once, no surrender and double any first 2 cards allowed (0.546 + 0.215 − 0.0137 = 0.7473) meaning that the house has three fourths of one percent advantage over a Basic Strategy player. Believe it or not, that fraction of a percent can add up quickly, because they have that advantage on every hand.

Let's say you plan to bet $10 a hand with no increases and you plan to play for 2 hours at a table with three other players. You will play about 120 hands and lose about $10 on average. In reality you will win some days and lose others, but in the long run, this is how it will play out. If you get a free drink or two you might even consider yourself ahead. Now consider that the casino has players betting $1,000 a hand or more and they are open 24/7 and you can see how they make money.

I only included the numbers for six deck games because the other games are very similar, and once you learn card-counting, *penetration* becomes a far more important a factor. Penetration is how far into the shoe the cards are dealt out before a shuffle is performed. The serious Blackjack player will want to have access to software that can calculate this for you. The best one I know of is **CVCX by QFIT.** You will see me refer to this software many times throughout this book, because I don't think it is possible to make a career of playing Blackjack without it or something very similar.

Typical Vegas Blackjack Rules

Here are the rules for the typical Las Vegas game. Six decks are dealt out of a shoe. The dealer hits soft-17 and stands at hard 17 or better. Double-after-split is allowed except if Aces are split. The player can split up to three times to make four hands with the exception of Aces which can only be split once. If Aces are split, the player will receive only one card for each Ace. If any other pair is split, the player will be able to stand, double, or split. Surrender is not offered.

Hopefully you have rid your mind of myths and are ready to learn to play like a machine. I have seen many players with the Basic Strategy card right in front of them, and do the exact opposite of what the card says. Occasionally I will ask them, "Are you sure that's what the card says?"

They reply, "No, the card says hit soft 18 against the nine, but every time I do, I make my hand worse and either bust, or lose with a hard 17."

That is exactly what will happen most of the time. In fact, every Basic Strategy decision fails more often than it succeeds. If it didn't the casino would not let you play with the strategy card in your hand. The house makes its hand last and for that reason the player loses most hands no matter how he plays.

Basic Strategy Chart for Las Vegas Strip Rules 4+ Decks (H17 DAS N S)

Player			Dealer	Up	Card					
Hard	2	3	4	5	6	7	8	9	10	Ace
4 - 8	H	H	H	H	H	H	H	H	H	H
9	H	Dh	Dh	Dh	Dh	H	H	H	H	H
10	Dh	Dh	Dh	Dh	Dh	Dh	Dh	Dh	H	H
11	Dh	Dh	Dh	Dh	Dh	Dh	Dh	Dh	Dh	Dh
12	H	H	S	S	S	H	H	H	H	H
13	S	S	S	S	S	H	H	H	H	H
14	S	S	S	S	S	H	H	H	H	H
15	S	S	S	S	S	H	H	H	H	H
16	S	S	S	S	S	H	H	H	H	H
17+	S	S	S	S	S	S	S	S	S	S
Soft	2	3	4	5	6	7	8	9	10	Ace
13	H	H	H	Dh	Dh	H	H	H	H	H
14	H	H	H	Dh	Dh	H	H	H	H	H
15	H	H	Dh	Dh	Dh	H	H	H	H	H
16	H	H	Dh	Dh	Dh	H	H	H	H	H
17	H	Dh	Dh	Dh	Dh	H	H	H	H	H
18	Ds	Ds	Ds	Ds	Ds	S	S	H	H	H
19	S	S	S	S	Ds	S	S	S	S	S
20+	S	S	S	S	S	S	S	S	S	S
Splits	2	3	4	5	6	7	8	9	10	Ace
2,2	P	P	P	P	P	P	H	H	H	H
3,3	P	P	P	P	P	P	H	H	H	H
4,4	H	H	H	P	P	H	H	H	H	H
6,6	P	P	P	P	P	H	H	H	H	H
7,7	P	P	P	P	P	P	H	H	H	H
8,8	P	P	P	P	P	P	P	P	P	P
9,9	P	P	P	P	P	S	P	P	S	S
Aces	P	P	P	P	P	P	P	P	P	P

H = Hit
S = Stand
Dh = Double if allowed, otherwise hit (can only double your first 2 cards)
Ds = Double if allowed, otherwise stand
P = Split

Before you learn to count you must know Basic Strategy, cold.

Basic Strategy can change depending on the rules of the Blackjack game that is being played. Casino Blackjack rules may vary. Professional Blackjack players know the rules of the casino before ever walking in the door. Games like Spanish 21, Double Exposure Blackjack, 21st-Century Blackjack,

Super Fun 21, Blackjack Switch, are considered carnival games and should not be confused with Blackjack or 21 as it is sometimes referred to. That is not to say that those games are without merit. They are simply beyond the scope of this book and require the use of a completely different Basic Strategy and card-counting techniques. You can go to our website www.darkstarBlackjack.com to find the Basic Strategy chart for any Blackjack game.

Whether the dealer hits or stands on a soft 17, is the rule that makes the most difference. Also, some casinos offer surrender, and you'll need to know exactly when to surrender. Surrender is technically a player advantage but many casinos offer it because, if it is overused, it favors the house.

Some of you will want to know why you should play according to Basic Strategy. Before I learned to play professionally, I played for fun. I thought I could improve on Basic Strategy just slightly. I reasoned that when the dealer shows a 7, she will have something other than a Ten or Ace, 8 out of 13 times, and will therefore have to draw. If I have a hard 16, 8 out of 13 times I will bust if I hit. Seems like I should let the dealer bust 8 out of 13 times rather than busting myself by the same ratio. While that may sound like solid math, it is flat wrong because it is over simplistic. Just because the dealer draws, does not mean she will bust, and I cannot assume I will bust by drawing on hard 16 either. There are many possibilities for my hand as well as the dealers that need to be considered.

That is how Basic Strategy was developed. The super computer of its day at the M.I.T. Computation Center was used by mathematicians in 1956 to develop the original Basic Strategy. Since then more powerful computers have been used to refine it for the modern game and all its variations.

If you want a more detailed explanation for how Basic Strategy was developed you are going to have to look up the original article which I sited in the very first sentence of this chapter. I trust most of you will be able to accept it as the least bad way to play your hand. At the time "Beat the Dealer" was published, it was the best way to play your hand, because

Basic Strategy alone gave the player a slight advantage over the house. Because of that book, Vegas changed the rules and casinos all over the world soon followed.

Currently, Basic Strategy alone will not give you an advantage over the house. This means that no matter how you play your hand, most of the time you will lose. You will simply lose less often by making the Basic Strategy play, than by playing any other way, assuming you are not counting-cards.

REMEMBER

Basic Strategy will not help you win more; it will help you lose less. Put simply, it is the least bad way to play. It is also the foundation for advantage play. The professional player needs to know Basic Strategy perfectly and without thinking about it and it is the way he will play his hand most of the time.

The Microwave Version of Basic Strategy

The basic logic applied in Basic Strategy is that since the dealer must draw on 16 or less and stand on 17 or more, the player should always hit on 16 or less when the dealer shows a 7 or better and stand on 12 or more when the dealer has less than a 7 showing. Then add three simple rules. Never take insurance or even money. Always double down on 11. Always split Aces and Eights. This is called the Microwave version of Basic Strategy. That's it! I'll explain all of these rules in more detail now but this one paragraph is the full Microwave version of Basic Strategy.

Let's examine the first part of this. For simplicity you should assume the hole-card is a Ten. Even though there is a greater chance (8 out of 13) that it is not a Ten. It could also be an Ace and that would still mean the dealer would not draw. That still leaves 7 out of 13 cards that would force the dealer to draw another card. At this point it gets a little complicated. There are a myriad of possibilities for the dealer's hand. She could have a 4 under the 7 and draw a Jack for 21. I could obviously go on and on but this is the Microwave version. So you just assume its a 10 and you need to have 17 or better to stand a chance at winning. You never hit Hard 17 because the odds of breaking outweigh the odds of the dealer getting 17 or better without busting.

The second part is easier to explain. You don't even have to assume the dealer's hole-card is a 10. No matter what card is under a dealer's Six or less, she will have to draw another card to reach at least 17 or bust. If the dealer has to hit, she might bust. So you should sit tight if there is any chance you could bust by taking a card.

Insurance is a bet that the dealer has Blackjack. Anytime the dealer has an Ace up she will offer insurance. You can bet up to half your original bet that the dealer's hole-card is a 10. If it is you will win 2:1 on your insurance bet and lose your original bet unless of course you also have Blackjack. If you have Blackjack and the dealer shows an Ace, in most casinos the the dealer will offer you even money. That means you can take a payment equal to your original wager and forgo the bonus.

Its called insurance because if you bet the maximum on insurance (½ your original wager) you will essentially push, losing the regular bet and winning double on the insurance bet. Don't be fooled by the name. Its a sucker bet and simply a bet that the card you cannot see is a ten. There are four tens (10, J, Q, K) and nine of everything else. So, if you make this bet 13 times you will win 4 times and lose 9 times on average. Since you get paid double, you'll get 8 units back for every 9 that you lose. Clearly the bet is in the houses favor. Why else would they offer it?

Even Money is exactly the same as insurance. Dealers and player will both try to tell you that its not the same but they're wrong. They're not lying, they're just wrong. If you have Blackjack and buy insurance no matter the outcome it is the same as taking even money. I'll let you go through the scenarios in your head if you don't believe me.

The only way you are going to get ahead in this game is by winning double downs and getting Blackjack once in a while. If you have 11 and double down, you are doubling your bet and getting just one more card. If this card is a 10 you have a hand that cannot be beat except by a dealer Blackjack but in that case you will only lose the original bet. So 4 out of 13 times you will end up with a total that can push at worst and 8 out of 13 times you will end up with a 17 or better. Since the dealer always tries to get 17 or more, that is the total to strive for. It makes sense to double your bet when you have a better than even chance of getting to your goal of 17.

The same logic applies to a pair of Aces. An Ace is eleven or one. So with two Aces you have 12 or 2. By splitting them you have two elevens. Just like when you double-down you are only going to get one additional card on each Ace. In some games, if the next card is another Ace, they make an exception and let you split again. That is a great rule for the player and you are obviously going to take advantage of it and split as many times as allowed.

If your first two cards are Eights, you will always split this into two hands. Depending on the rules, you may or may not be able to double-after-split. If you get a 3 for your next card on either 8, you will follow the always double 11 rule if they let you. If you get any other card, you will hit or stand based on the rules above.

The full Basic Strategy is far more complicated than this but I think it helps to first understand this condensed version. That way you understand the logic behind Basic Strategy. Since the casino will actually let you consult a Basic Strategy card before making a decision on your hand, I see no reason not to go beyond the Microwave Version.

Learning Basic Strategy

Different people learn in different ways. What worked for me was to make flash cards. On one side I put my hand and on the other I wrote the correct play for every dealer up card. You can go to my website www.darkstarBlackjack.com for a Basic Strategy chart and set of flash cards for the particular game you are playing.

For me, it's easier to remember what to do with each hand against all the various dealer cards, and make it into a sentence. If you already understand the logic behind the Microwave Version of Basic Strategy, you can turn all of the Basic Strategy plays into sentences. I.E., split 7s against 2-7, or split nines against 2 – 9, except 7. In the latter, you should be good enough to know that you would never hit a hard 18, no matter what the dealer has. Likewise, you should know what to do with a 14, if you're not splitting the 7s, by simply applying the microwave rule.

If you ultimately decide not to go any further than basic strategy for any number reasons, just understand that you will be playing to lose as little as possible rather than to win. For 7 down and dirty tactics to improve your Blackjack game, check out our blog post: 7 Steps to Improved Blackjack Strategy

2   Don Schlesinger. Blackjack Attack: Playing the Pros' Way (North Las Vegas: RGE Publishing, Ltd, 2005)

♠ Chapter 4 - Advantage Play

I don't like to call it card counting because that sounds like you are either counting the number of cards being dealt or keeping track of exactly how many of each card is dealt. Instead you are simply keeping track of the ratio of small cards (2-6 or 3-6) to big cards (10, J, Q, K, A). By knowing this information, a player can monitor and adjust his/her bet in accordance with the cards that have a greater than average chance of being dealt. How does a player determine this? The player simply assigns a value to all of the cards. For most count systems 7,8 and 9 are assigned a value of 0 and are basically ignored. You need to do this for all of the cards dealt. Not just yours and the dealer's. This is no easy task and will require many hours of practice at home, but most people are capable of learning how to count-cards, provided they put in the required effort.

If, after reading this book, you decide card-counting is too much work and just want to reduce the house edge when you play for fun, I'll give you a hint. Keep this in mind when you play. Progressive bettors are playing exactly backwards in most cases. I cover progressive betting in a separate chapter. When the progressive bettor wins with a twenty and other players are winning with Blackjack and 19 or the dealer is busting by drawing a ten on her 15 or 16 starting hand, he increases his bet. Twenties and Blackjacks come out again and again he increases his wager. Does this make sense? Is it likely more Faces and Aces are going to come out of that shoe? Not unless the cards are behaving like rabbits and reproducing in the back of that shoe. Eventually the small cards have to come out. The opposite is true as well. If the entire table is losing because the dealer can't seem to bust and draws small card after small card to make a hand and you are being dealt cards like 6, 3, 7, 6, now what is left in that shoe? More of the same because cards are like rabbits, right?

That is not the only way you can win or lose, of course, but it is the most common. So think of it like the stock market. You want to buy low i.e. when you are losing and sell high i.e. when you are winning. In the case of Blackjack, buying means increasing your wager and selling means reducing it. Don't get me wrong. This is not a short cut to advantage play. Advantage play means you have the advantage instead of the house. In this case, you are still at a disadvantage, only less so. To truly beat the house most of the time, you will have to put in the hard work of learning to count cards and play according to the count.

There are various card counting systems that a player can learn with frequent and continual practice. The Hi-Lo Count System is the most commonly used Blackjack card counting system.

The Hi-Lo Count System

In simplest terms, here is a table that shows the values for all the cards in a deck.

2, 3, 4, 5, 6	7, 8, 9	10, J, Q, K, A
+1	0	-1

By examining the table, you can see that there are an equal number of cards whose value equals +1 (Five cards—2 through 6) as cards that equal -1 (Five cards—10 through Ace). So, if you take out a deck of cards, and start counting them using the above method, when you get to the end of the deck, you should always end at zero. The same goes with multiple decks. If you are counting, say, three decks of cards, your total value should end at zero by the end of the third deck.

Practice Activity

1.) Take a deck of cards and shuffle it.

2.) Remove one card and place it face down.

3.) Using the Hi-Lo count, begin counting the value of all of the cards in the deck.

4.) When you reach the end of the deck, if your count is +1, then the remaining card should be a ten valued card (10, Jack, Queen, or King) or an Ace. Likewise, if your count is -1, your remaining card should be a 2, 3, 4, 5, or 6. And, if your count ends at zero, then your remaining card should be a 7, 8, or 9.

This is excellent practice that you must do if you want to be a good card-counter. Don't worry about speed at first. Accuracy is more important. However, eventually you will need to be able to count as fast or faster than a dealer can deal.

Before I go into any casino, I make sure I can go through three decks perfectly. Eventually you want to be able to count cards pretty fast. Your goal should be to be able to count almost as fast as you can flip through the cards without dropping them all over the floor.

Card-Counting Vision

I know this will sound strange, sort of like hocus-pocus, but there will come a time, after countless hours, and days, and weeks, and months of practice, when you will be sitting in a casino some fine day, and you will realize, through some kind of mental-metamorphosis, that you can just "see" the card count by looking at a table full of cards. It comes that fast. This "revelation," if you want to call it that, came to me after about 9 months of continuous card counting and several trips to the casino. In the meantime, you will just have to work hard keeping the totals in your head through hard work and persistence.

What Is The Point?

Learning to count-cards, and count them well—accurately and fast—is where the payoff comes. Just counting cards by itself gains you nothing. It's how you use that information that will put money in your bank account.

Higher the Count/Higher the Bet

Now stop and think about that. The higher the count total, the more you should bet. Why is that so? A high positive count means that a lot of 2s, 3s, 4s, 5s, and 6s have hit the table. So what is remaining in the deck or the shoe? Basic probability will tell you that there are NOW more 10s, Jacks, Queens, Kings, and Aces left to be dealt. Ten-valued cards and Aces favor the player for several reasons. Of course you will be more likely to get good hands but so will the dealer. The difference is that if you get a Blackjack, you will win 1 and a half what you bet. If the dealer gets a Blackjack you will only lose what you bet. Also, doubling down on tens and elevens will be more likely to result in a total of 21. In fact, when the count is high you should double and split more often than Basic Strategy recommends. Finally, the dealer is required to hit till he/she gets to 17 or better. The player can use information about the cards remaining to stand on stiffs more often. A stiff is a hand with a lousy hard total like 15 or 16. I'll get into more detail on that later.

How high should you raise your bet?

The answer to this questions depends on a lot of factors. How much is your bankroll? How much risk are you willing to take? Are you concerned about attracting too much attention from the floor manager by "jumping your bet?" In fact there is so much that goes into this question that I had to dedicate an entire chapter to it. I only bring it up here, as a tease, because this seems to be the burning question on student's minds.

Lower the Count/Lower the Bet

So it makes sense if the count is -16, that there are a lot of low cards waiting to come out. These are hands that will typically bring defeat, so you want to lower your bet to minimize your losses. Even if we are talking about running counts, once you get to double digit negative, you should consider lowering your bet to zero. In fact, my first advantage play instructor and I had a motto, "If you get to M16 walk away before you get shot down." We counted negative numbers in our head by putting M in front of the numeral. Like M1, M2, etc. because it is much faster and easier than thinking negative 1, negative 2. The odds of a count climbing back to positive territory before the end of the shoe after reaching M16 are about the same as escaping from a mine field with Arnold Schwarzenegger firing an M-16 at you.

If you already play a lot of Blackjack just for recreation, you'll be amazed at how much sense 8 card 21's for the dealer will actually make once you learn a count system. Try not to laugh at the other players when they say, "The damn dealer drew 6 cards and couldn't find a single Ten! Where the hell are the Tens!". You'll be thinking, are we at the same table? 25 ten-valued cards, five Aces and only six cards that were 3-6 hit the table before we saw the dealer's cards on this hand! Since this is double-deck, we only have 7 more Tens and one more Ace (because the dealer drew 2 Aces) and we won't play all of the cards. It would actually be a surprise to see a Ten now but you'll be the only one betting table minimum on that last hand. Parlaying winnings is the most common strategy used by all gamblers. I described earlier how cards are not rabbits but many people play as if they were. Believe it or not that was almost the exact scenario I saw play out one time. The dealer's hand was 3, 2, 3, 4, Ace, Ace, 2, 5.

True Count

If you've done the practice you might be able to keep the running count while playing now. You are not even close to being able to play with an advantage over the house at this point. If you try it and lose big, remember I warned you. In fact, you might do more harm than good at this point because as the saying goes, "There is nothing more dangerous than a little knowledge." Without the whole picture you could easily lose more than you would by just guessing how much to bet.

The true count is the running count divided by the number of decks remaining in the shoe. So if train A leaves the station traveling at... Just kidding! This is the most difficult math you will have to do. The precision you use on this calculation will depend on how quickly you can divide by fractions and how good your eye sight is. First you need to know how many decks are left. To do this you first need to know how many you started with. Sounds funny but you'd be surprised how many people I meet that claim to be able to count cards and then say something like, "five decks, right?" when its actually eight being used. You could simply ask the dealer how many decks are used. But if you practice what I teach you here, you'll be able easily determine this on your own.

The best way to determine the number of decks remaining is by looking at the discard rack.

Obviously the casino will not make it this easy by stacking boxes of cards next to it. I did this so you can clearly see there are two decks in the discard rack and if we are playing out of a six deck shoe as suggested here, there are 4 decks left. So far my six year old can easily follow the math. A word of caution – just because the discard rack can hold six decks does not mean six decks are being used. Many casinos, including the one I work at use eight deck discard trays on six deck games. In addition they slant the discard tray slightly to make it harder to see how many cards are in there.

If you plan to play mostly six deck shoes and either think you will have a hard time estimating the number of decks to a precision greater than the nearest whole number or you just don't want to divide by fractions, stick to that. Remember playing with as few mistakes as possible is far more important than anything else. If you are playing a double-deck game, you'll want to be a little more precise. I'd say estimating to the nearest half deck is sufficient.

With enough practice, you should be able to estimate the number of decks dealt out to within half a deck even with all of the optical illusions the casino will throw at you. Enoch was able to estimate it to within a ¼ deck and when we practiced he could tell me to within 1 or 2 the exact number of cards left in a six deck shoe. There are a couple of different ways to practice. One is by rubber banding a few different stacks of cards. Make one a half deck, one ¾ of deck and maybe another that is a full deck. Have a partner show you one of the groups and see if you can identify it. This is a good way to start. You should do this from a distance that is close to what you'll experience in a casino. Once proficient at that you can combine 6 decks and grab a random amount. Guess how many you have and then count. There is also software that can help you practice this. In fact, I highly recommend anyone who is even a little serious about playing Blackjack profitably purchase Casino Verite Blackjack from QFIT. It is the best Blackjack practice software available. You can select the type of count you are using. Customize a strategy. Select the table conditions for the casino you'll be playing at and many other variables. It will let you know when you make an error either in betting or playing your hand. I am not affiliated with them and as of this writing have no financial agreement with them. I'm not promoting their product for any reason other than to help improve your game.

Once you know how many decks are left, divide your running count by that number. If we were looking at the tray in the picture above and we had a running count of 8 we would have a true count of 2. That was too easy you say. What if the running count was 13? Then 13 / 4 = 3.25. For practical purposes you would round this down to 3. If the true count was 14, you could consider rounding up to 4. That depends on your risk tolerance.

Personally, I truncate rather than round to the nearest whole number. For this example I'd be betting at the 3 level unless the running count was at least 16. There are two reasons I do this. One, it's easier. Since I know 16 / 4 is 4 and 12 / 4 is 3, I don't have to do the math exactly. More than 12 but less than 16 with 4 decks left is going to be whatever I bet at 3. Secondly, because maintaining my bankroll is more important than squeezing every last dollar from the game. It is less risky to round down than up. For simplicity I apply the same principle to decisions about my hand and when to deviate from basic strategy. That will be discussed in the next section.

First, let's think about a double-deck game. If you are going to play double-deck, please find a good one. Most double-deck games only deal out one deck before they shuffle up. As you'll see in the chapter on selecting a game, that is probably not a game worth playing. But if you find a double-deck game where they deal till half a deck or less is left and you still get paid 3 to 2 on Blackjack, you'll want to be able to estimate to within at least half a deck. Quarter deck would be great. This is easier than you might think in a double-deck game. You'll actually get a feel for it without even looking at the discard tray because even with just a couple of players the dealer will be shuffling after less than 10 rounds. Because I'm not great at math, I just estimate to within half a deck. If you can easily see that a running count of 3 with 1 ½ decks left is a true count of 2 then you are in good shape.

When NOT to Use Basic Strategy

I had hard 15 against the dealer's Ten. Basic strategy requires me to hit. However, the count was more than plus 4. So, I stood. I'm not thinking of a specific time because this exact scenario has happened more times than I can count – pun intended. Many times I lost because the dealer had 17 or better but would have lost anyway because the next card out was 7 or more. Very often the dealer had a six or less under the Ten, was required to hit and busted with a Ten. In the above example and in all examples in this book, when I refer to the count, I am referring to the true count unless otherwise stated.

Depending where you are in the game, how many decks are left in the shoe, what the count is, etc., will determine things like whether you will hit or stand on a certain play. It will also determine when to split or double-down, and if you take insurance or surrender. Nothing is left to chance. There is mathematics behind almost every move you make in a game.

There are at least 165 deviations to Basic Strategy, where you will NOT play as the Basic Strategy card recommends, rather you should alter your game play according to the true count. I do not recommend that anybody memorize all 165 Basic Strategy exceptions, unless you have a head shaped like an alien or a football. In other words, you are a super-brianiac. WINK!

I don't know all 165 like Professor Schlesinger. All you really need to know are Don Schlesinger's "Illustrious 18." There are 18 situations that come up often and make the most difference. This is the list that many professional Blackjack players use and that I recommend. I know a few more than the 18, and I use them just because I happen to know them, but it's not important. If you follow Basic Strategy, except for these 18 deviations, you will be playing a very, very good game of Blackjack, and you will make money in the long run. I prefer the Hi-Opt I with an Ace side count to Hi-Lo and Don Schlesinger uses the Revere Point Count but published the Illustrious 18 based on Hi-Lo because it is the most used count system and the differences in the count systems for purposes of this chart are not statistically significant. Remember that this is a science but not an exact science. We are working with probabilities and making the best decision for long term results. In any given situation basic strategy may have worked better. In fact, if you don't think you can memorize all of these perfectly, you are better off using Basic Strategy regardless of the count. In fact, you could play with a Basic Strategy card in your hand or on the table in front of you. Just use the count to adjust your wager. This may have the added benefit of allowing you to play at your favorite casino every day without being barred. Pit bosses and surveillance will not consider a player using a basic strategy card as a serious threat especially if you always do what the card suggests. I'll get into that in more detail in the chapter on camouflage.

Here is The Illustrious 18 taken from Don Schlesinger's *Blackjack Attack 3rd Edition Chapter 5* except I changed the order they are listed in. You follow the Action advise when the true count is equal to or greater than the Index # for the positive index numbers and less than or equal to for the negative index numbers, otherwise you follow Basic Strategy.

Total V Dealer	Index # (True Count)	Action	Basic Strategy
Insurance	>= 3	Take Insurance	Pass
16 V 10	>= 0	STAND	HIT
16 V 9	>= 5	STAND	HIT
15 V 10	>= 4	STAND	HIT
12 v 3	>= 2	STAND	HIT
12 V 2	>= 3	STAND	HIT
9 V 2	>= 1	DOUBLE DOWN	HIT
9 V 7	>= 3	DOUBLE DOWN	HIT
10 V 10	>= 4	DOUBLE DOWN	HIT
10 V ACE	>= 4	DOUBLE DOWN	HIT
11 V ACE	>= 1	DOUBLE DOWN	HIT
12 V 4	<= 0	HIT	STAND
12 V 5	<= -2	HIT	STAND
12 V 6	<= -1	HIT	STAND
13 V 3	<= -3	HIT	STAND
13 V 2	<= -1	HIT	STAND
10,10 V 6	>= 4	DOUBLE DOWN	STAND
10,10 V 5	>= 5	DOUBLE DOWN	STAND

This is the way it was easiest for me to memorize. I saved the ten splits for last for the same reason Don almost called it the Sweet 16 and left those two out. One reason is camouflage. I dedicate an entire chapter to that subject later but I'll just touch on it here. The casino knows that only three kinds of people split tens. New players, card counters and immature drunks who want to show off. So if you are playing Basic Strategy most of the time without looking at a strategy card and appear sober, there is only one other explanation. Being identified as a card-counter is not a good thing for reasons I'll cover later.

If you are playing in a casino that offers surrender, Don Schlesinger created and published the "Fab Four" surrenders in the same book. Surrender means that you can give up half your bet if you do not like your first two cards. This can only be done with the first two cards and usually only after the dealer checks to see if she has Blackjack. This is referred to as late surrender. Basic Strategy will tell you to surrender 15 against a dealer Ten and 16 against a 9 or 10. Here are the "Fab Four" variations to that.

First 2 Vs Dealer	Surrender if Index is >=
14 V 10	3
15 V 10	0 *this means don't surrender if negative count*
15 V 9	2
15 V ACE	1

The Illustrious 18 and Fab 4 are well known to all serious advantage players. The software I mentioned earlier will allow you to set your strategy to the Illustrious 18 and Fab 4 or the full index. It will even adjust this depending on the count system you are using and has every count system I have ever heard of in its data base. If you choose not to use the software you can just make the best decision and then check the chart to see if you were right. I should point out that winning or losing the hand has nothing to do with it. In fact, if you make the wrong decision and win, it does not make it right any more than it would be right to rob a bank as long as you didn't get caught. If you plan to play for the long term and make a living or even supplement your income you will need to make the right decision every time and even if it fails ten times in a row, know that you are doing the right thing.

The next chapter explains the Hi-Opt I with Ace Side Count System that I personally use. If you plan to stick with Hi-Lo for now, you can skip this chapter. You may want to put the book down for few days or more either now or after the next chapter and start practicing. Practice at HOME! Not in the casino. I have not even answered the vital question on how much to bet. This is deliberate. You need to walk before you can run. Learn from my mistakes. I got this far in my initial training. I spent months counting down decks and going through flash cards till I knew Basic Strategy and the Illustrious 18 inside and out forward and back. I hit the casinos with a few thousand bucks and decided to make up the betting strategy on the fly. The result was about the same as a toddler attempting to run as soon as he could just barely stand upright.

♡Chapter 5 - The Next Level

Basic card counting assigns a positive, negative, or zero value to each card value available. When a card of that value is dealt, the count is adjusted by that card's counting value. Low cards increase the count as they increase the percentage of high cards in the remaining shoe, while high cards decrease it for the opposite reason. For instance, the Hi-Lo system subtracts one for each dealt ten, Jack, Queen, King or Ace, and adds one for any 2-6. Cards 7-9 are assigned a value of zero and therefore do not affect the count.

The goal of a card counting system is to assign point values that roughly correlate to a card's Effect of Removal (EOR). The EOR is the actual effect of removing a given card from play, and the resulting impact on the house advantage. The player may gauge the effect of removal for all cards dealt, and assess the current house advantage of a game based on the remaining cards. As larger ratios between point values are used to create better correlation to actual EOR with the goal of increasing the efficiency of a system, such systems use larger and larger numbers and are broken into classes such as level 1, level 2, level 3, and so on, with regard to the ratio between the highest and lowest assigned point values. [1.]

The Hi-Lo system is considered a *single-level* or *level-one* count, because the count never increases or decreases by more than a single, predetermined value. A *multilevel* count, such as *Zen Count* or *Wong Halves*, makes finer distinctions between card values to gain greater play accuracy. Rather than all cards having a value of +1, 0, or −1, an advanced count might also include card ranks that are counted as +2 and −2, or +0.5. Advanced players might additionally maintain a *side count* (separate count) of specific cards, such as a side count Aces, to deal with situations where the best count for betting accuracy differs from the best count for playing accuracy.

Many side count techniques exist including special-purpose counts used when attacking games with nonstandard profitable-play options such as an over/under side bet. [2.]

The disadvantage of higher-level counts is that keeping track of more information can detract from the ability to play quickly and accurately. If you make more mistakes by using a more complex count system, you will definitely make more money with a simpler system. You should use the most effective system that you can without making any mistakes. You need to be very close to perfect.

If you make a play error, like hitting when you should stand, it only affects that hand. However, a mistake in the count affects all the rest of the hands until the end of the shoe. This can be very costly. Being off by 1 card usually won't hurt you that much but two or more could be disastrous. Let's say you are keeping a running count and dividing by the number of decks remaining to get the true count. So if the count is -1 after 3 rounds in a six deck game but you think it's +1, when you get to the last few rounds the true count might be +2 and you have it at +4.

First off, you will be betting two or three times more than you should. Then to make it worse, you will make the wrong decision on your 15 vs. the dealer's Jack, and stand when you should have taken the 6 of Hearts waiting for you. If you now lose $400 when you should have won $200, it negatively impacts your bankroll by $600 and you still have a couple of hands left.

The worst part is, you won't even know you made the mistake. This is one reason you need to practice at home and keep track of how many errors you are making. Don't go into a casino until you can play perfectly at home. If you make mistakes in the privacy and quiet of your den, what will happen in a noisy casino filled with more distractions than you can imagine?

Hi-Opt I with Ace Side-count

One mistake I made early on was trying to use one count system for one type of game and another for a different game.

At that time my two favorite casinos were near each other in Minnesota. Actually, relatively close for Midwestern casinos. It was an hour drive or so between casinos. I like to keep a side count of Aces especially in double or single-deck games. The Ace is the only card that can have two different values. Not only that, but you need an Ace to get a Natural or Blackjack. For these reasons I never thought it made sense to treat the Ace the same as a Ten. The easiest count I knew of that did not assign the same value to an Ace as a Ten was Hi-Opt I. Since it actually assigns a value of 0 to the Ace, it is necessary, in my opinion, to keep a side count of Aces when using this count. That was the ideal count for the double- deck game. However, I thought it would be too difficult to keep a side count while playing the six deck game an hour away. So I used Hi-Lo on the six deck game and Hi-Opt I with an Ace side count on the double-deck game.

It's difficult to know with certainty how many mistakes I made, but I'm sure I made enough to negate any advantage the more advanced count gave me. I have since developed a system that makes keeping the Ace count easier for four to eight deck shoe games. I'll describe that in a little while. For now, the point is, pick a system that works for you and stick with it. If you later decide to make a change, apply that change unilaterally.

Hi-Opt I assigns a value of +1 to 3-6 and a value of -1 to all Tens. 2, 7, 8, 9 and Ace are ignored.

3, 4, 5, 6	2, 7, 8, 9, A	10, J, Q, K
+1	0	-1

Hi-Opt is short for highly optimal in case you're curious—a bold claim for a single-level count. While there are professional players using complicated multilevel counts without errors, research has proven that these systems do not offer any significant advantage. So I see no reason for a new player to learn them. Even with an Ace side count Hi-Opt I is still a single-level count.

I count the Aces with letters to keep the two counts separate. If I see J, Q, 3, 5, A, 6, 3, A the count is 2-B--four small cards minus 2 big cards and 2 Aces. The important thing to understand is how many extra Aces or fewer Aces are left in the deck than you would expect. If that represented the first 8 cards that were dealt, the deck is definitely Ace poor now. Since there are 4 Aces in a 52 card deck, we will see 1 Ace every 13 cards on average. We now have roughly 1 ½ less Aces to give us Blackjacks and other good outcomes. So what? So, for betting purposes we subtract 1 from our running count. You could subtract 1 ½ but few people can make exact calculations in the heat of the moment. So, in this case, 2-B means that I am only able to bet at a running count level of 1, not 2.

As for the illustrious 18, you would use the UN-adjusted count of 2 with the exceptions of splitting tens and double down on 10 or 9. Being short on Aces means you will want to use more caution on these plays. This works well in a double-deck game. For example, you have a running count of 4-G going into the last hand. It's a very well penetrated game meaning that 1 ¼ decks have been dealt out already. Your betting schedule is $10 at 0-1, $25 at 2, $50 at 3, $75 at 4, $100 at 5+. What do you bet? G means you have seen 7 Aces but in 1 ¼ decks, you should have only seen 5. Therefore, running count of 4 - 2 extra Aces = 2. Then divide by ¾ of a deck to get closer to 3 than 2. You don't need to be any more precise than that.

I told you earlier that I err on the side of caution. That means I should bet $25 here because I would not round 2.66 up to 3. However, there is an advanced mathematical principle called the floating point advantage that Don Schlesinger originally proposed and Peter Griffin proved. That math is complicated so I am not going to go into it. Suffice it to say that you have a greater advantage than normal when you have less than a deck remaining. In this case, anything greater than 2 could be rounded up to 3 because of the floating point advantage. That means a bet of $50. Either way, you need to bet less than $75 (amount if not adjusting for Aces). Of course this works in the reverse direction as well. Had the count been 4-A, I would bet $100 and hope for a chance to double-down on 10 since at least one of the 7 Aces left has a good chance of coming out on the last hand. Try to laugh it off when the dealer flips over Blackjack for herself.

Most professional players do not attempt a side-count of Aces with 6 or more decks but I devised a very easy way to do this. I buy ten white ($1) chips from the dealer. They won't question you on this because they'll assume they are for tips. That means you should use one or two for that purpose. The rest you will use to keep track of the number of Aces dealt out. Remember I count them using letters. So every time I get to D, I drop a white chip down and make a small stack of them. Then I start back at A. What's great about this is that you can easily see how the number of Aces dealt compares to the number of decks dealt. If you have a short stack of 3 white chips and 3 decks are in the discard tray then you are at even plus your letter count.

If this is what you have in front of you, consider alternating and using green or red for the next round.

Just be smart about when and how you do this. The house knows that some card-counters use chips to keep the count. Wait until after the round to drop your next white chip on the stack and I would think about dropping one on the stack and tossing one to the dealer as a tip at the same time. This will make you look less like a card-counter because from the house's perspective card-counters are jerks who don't tip. Also, it will put the focus on the tip, even if it's only a dollar, and might get the dealer to worry less about whether or not you're counting-cards.

Even if they figure out that you are counting Aces with your chips, you'll not be seen as much of a threat. Using an Ace count alone may give you a slight advantage but you won't always be increasing your bet when there is a shortage of Aces. If you look like you are tracking the Aces but using the information incorrectly, you'll be exactly what the house wants – a moron who thinks she's a genius!

Remember, the most important thing is to be accurate with whatever system you use. If this is too difficult to do with all of the distractions of a casino, stick to Hi-Lo. You will not be giving up that much profit or adding very much extra risk. In the next chapter I talk about how much to bet based on your bankroll. If you can't see your bankroll ever increasing beyond $25,000, then you will not be missing much by giving up on the Ace side count. The Hi-Opt I count is almost as good as Hi-Lo on its own. Since you are assigning a value to less cards, it is an easier count system without the Ace side-count. For that reason it is prudent to learn Hi-Opt I and use it when you start and add the Ace count later, as your bankroll increases. I only included the chapter on Hi-Lo because so many people are already familiar with it and any professional player should at least be familiar with it.

1. Axelrad, Josh (2010). *Repeat until Rich: A Professional Card Counter's Chronicle of the Blackjack Wars*. New York: Penguin Press. ISBN 978-1-59420-247-6.

2. https://www.qfit.com/Blackjack-side-counts.htm

♣Chapter6 - Betting Strategy and Bankroll

You may wish to determine what your bankroll is going to be. In order to do that, you need to define what a bankroll is. I define bankroll as the amount of money that you have available to play Blackjack. Sounds simple enough, yes? Well it might not be that simple. Bankroll does not include money that you need for expenses. So, for example, let's say that you have $10,000 to play Blackjack and you live in Chicago and you want to play Blackjack in Las Vegas. You won't be able to play Blackjack assuming you're going to pay $500 on air fare and $200 on hotel and $100 for dinner and $150 on a hooker because you just depleted your bankroll by $950. So your bankroll is just the money used for playing Blackjack only and the expenses that you incur have to come out of a separate account set aside just for that—paying your expenses.

So how much bankroll do you need? Well this is the big question and depends on a lot of things. First, you need to figure out whether playing Blackjack is going to be your primary source of income, or do you have a job or another source of income so that you don't have to live off of playing Blackjack?

Risk of Ruin

There is a term called **risk of ruin**, which is the percentage of risk of losing your entire bankroll. If you were playing professionally and playing Blackjack was your only income, you would not want your risk of ruin to be greater than 1%. If, however, playing Blackjack is for entertainment purposes or is supplemental income, then the risk of ruin number can be as high as you choose, depending on your tolerance for risk. So if you are willing to accept 10% risk, which means there is a 10% chance of losing your entire bankroll, and you could live with that because you could just simply wait until you save up another bankroll again, then that's a decision you have to make and feel comfortable with.

Something to consider when playing Blackjack is, if you are going to play the game as your primary source of income, then you should also be prepared for plenty of long dry spells. It's not unusual or unheard of to go two or three months without making a single profit. So, you have to have other money set aside to live on, or you have to have the ability to borrow money to live on. As a rule of thumb, you should be prepared to go three months without making enough profit to live on. You could even lose for 3 months in a row. Personally, I have never lost for more than 1 month at a time, but that doesn't mean that it's not possible. A bad streak for me was when I had a month where I lost, then broke even the following month, then lost in the next month. Well that's not much different than losing three months in a row. So having two or three bad months can happen and you have to be prepared for that.

Another consideration for how big your bankroll should be is whether you plan on playing alone, or with a team. Are you going to try and set up a Blackjack team like the M.I.T. people did? I will get into how to set up a Blackjack team in a later chapter.

Method of Play

There are a few ways to attack a Blackjack table. You can sit down at the start of the shoe and just play all of the hands regardless of the count. That is called Play-All. You can decide that you will walk away from a table when the count drops below a certain level, known as "Wonging-out". When the running count gets below -9 it is very unlikely to get back to a high enough count to put the edge in favor of the player before the end of the shoe. If its six decks and it happens within the first three rounds, you might want to give it a hand or two to recover. You can also "Wong-in" or back-count the shoe. That means that you stand near the table and watch the cards being dealt without playing. When the count gets to a predetermined level you jump in and play. It helps if you do this from the start of the shoe but you technically don't have to. Unseen cards are unseen cards. So, if you started watching the table and one out of six decks was already dealt, you would divide the running count by five instead of six to get the true count after the first round you observe. Just remember to adjust for that deck when you look at the discard tray as you go. Now you see why I said it helps if you do it from the start. That's too much work for me. I'd rather find a table where the dealer is starting to shuffle. Work smarter not harder.

You can combine all of these methods in the same trip. Maybe you "Wong-in" to the first table and stay as long as it doesn't dip below -9. Then play the start of the next shoe. If the count starts off good, you stay. If the first round produces four Blackjacks for the players and one for the dealer as well, you might want to get up. Everyone will think you are just superstitious but the real reason is with that many Tens and Aces gone in the first round, what's the point? It's called Wonging, by the way, because it was first described by Stanford Wong, one of the greatest Blackjack players of all time. He wrote several excellent books on the subject all published under the pen name Stanford Wong. He was born John Ferguson in 1943 and was still playing Blackjack when he wrote the books.

You should decide ahead of time which method or methods you are going to use. This is where software can help you. There is some very specific software called CVCX that I recommend from QFIT, the same company that makes the excellent Casino Verite Blackjack software. Essentially CVCX is Casino Verite Chapter 10 (X) of Don Schlessinger's excellent book, Blackjack Attack · . I am not too full of myself to tell you that Blackjack Attack should be a part of your Blackjack reading library. The people at QFIT came up with a whole program that will simulate gaming situations that you enter. For example, you tell CVCX how you want to play, what count system you are using, how much you are going to bet in specific circumstances, what your bankroll is, etc., and then it plays Blackjack hands over-and-over again, against an imaginary casino dealer, and you tell it how many times you are going to do this. You will run this simulation at least 50 million times and it will run the program playing 50 million hands overnight at the parameters you have established. I run it for about 100 million hands, and even if you have a computer with a super-fast multi-core processor, it will take several hours to run. Once the simulation is completed you can adjust your bets to see what your risk will be and your expected win rate. You can click on a back-count button and set the level at which you will enter the table. The program will assume you will leave when the count drops below that level as well, unless a new version came out after this was written that lets you set a Wong-out level as well.

Casino House Rules

Another consideration is where you are playing. Are you playing a single-deck game? Are you playing a double- deck game? Are you playing a 6 deck game? Does the dealer stand on soft 17? Does the dealer hit all 17s? Can you double any first two cards? Are you getting paid 3 to 2 on Blackjack? All of these rules will have an effect on what your bankroll should be.

So, let's say for an example that you are one player, playing alone, and you're going to play all the hands, and you have a $10,000 bankroll, and this is supplementary income where you play on the side and just make some extra money and have some fun. In this particular scenario, you would be able to make $14 an hour with a 2.4% risk of ruin, if you found a double-deck game with a table minimum of $10 and decent penetration. Here is what your betting strategy would look like:

True Count	Bet
<= +1	10
+2	25
+3	50
>= +4	75

Now what would happen if you only added 50% to your bankroll using this same scenario? So instead of playing with a $10,000 bankroll, you now have a $15,000 bankroll. The resulting bump in bankroll will now allow you to more than double your hourly rate and cut your risk by almost half or 46%. The result is $28 per hour with a 1.3% risk of ruin. A 1.3% risk of ruin is acceptable for even a professional Blackjack player. Most professionals will want you to keep their risk of ruin under 1% so you might want a little extra cushion but I would take the extra risk. If $28 an hour is acceptable to you, all you need is $15,000. Here is your betting schedule for that scenario:

True Count	Bet
<= 0	10
+1	25
+2	50
+3	75
+4	100
+5	125
>=+6	150

If you think you could live on $28 an hour, and you had $20,000 you can make a nice living. I say 20K because I am adding $5,000 for expenses. Remember, the bankroll is only for playing Blackjack. You still have to buy airfare or gas, food, lodging, tips for dealers and waitresses. You always have to be prepared for up to 3 months with no income. You need separate money to live on besides the $20,000, or you would need to have the ability to borrow it against credit cards or savings if you had to.

Obviously you are planning on becoming a gambler so you will likely be willing to take on a certain amount of risk.

Here is another example. It happens to be at one of my favorite casinos that has a Blackjack game I love.

4 Decks

Table Minimum: $25

Table Max: $500

Rules: Players can split up to three times to make up to four hands, even if you have Aces. However, you only get one card if you split Aces. You can double-after-split except Aces. Late surrender is allowed—ability to surrender your hand if you don't like the first two cards you are dealt only after the dealer checks for Blackjack. You can double anything, great penetration. They deal 3 decks out of 4, sometimes even more than that.

Pro Level 1% Risk of Ruin for this game to make $56/hour, would require a bankroll of $35,000 plus expenses.

The bets would look like this:

True Count	Bet
<= 0	25
+1	50
+2	125
+3	200
+4	275

At most casinos that big of a spread would draw heat. As long as you use a reasonable amount of camouflage, you could play here for a long time. Your $56 an hour might drop to around $50 because you would not raise after a push and many times you would bet $100 at +2 instead of $125. As of this writing, they are not overly concerned about card-counters because they assume there are very few of them who are any good and it cost more to thwart them than its worth. If enough of you read this and play there, that might change which is why I didn't mention the name of the casino. I'm sure there are other casinos that are so enlightened. Finding out what you can get away with is what makes this job fun.

The Kelly Criterion

Something you will see if you get this software is the Kelly Criterion. This is one of those things that you have to understand if you want to consider yourself a professional gambler or investor even if you never use the information. Does an accountant need to know that Alexander Hamilton established the Treasury to do your taxes? Do you think there are any CPA s worth their salt that don't know that? The Kelly Criterion was created by John Kelly who worked at AT&T's Bell Laboratory. It was developed to assist with long distance telephone signal noise issues. It was quickly seen as a powerful math tool for gambling and investing. I'm not sure there is a difference there but I digress. The equation looks like this:

Producti $[(1+wixi)^{(n*pi)}] - 1$,

where:
wi is the net payout for the ith outcome
xi the stake for the ith outcome
pi the probability of the ith outcome. [1.]

If that makes sense to you and you want to use it, more power to you. Just remember that betting true Kelly means adjusting your bet every time your bankroll goes up or down. If you adjusted every time your bankroll declined, you would, in theory, never lose the entire bankroll. In practice it might become impossible to bet .05% of $100 if that was all that was left in your bankroll. You do the math. For that reason most gamblers who use this method wager a fraction of true Kelly. Most recommend betting half Kelly. You could then adjust at the end of every trip if there was a significant change in your bankroll.

I no longer use the Kelly Criterion. I find it much easier to adjust my bets in the software to achieve a risk of ruin level I can live with and a win rate that is acceptable. I can adjust for swings in the bankroll at the end of every trip or as they occur.

For you, the easiest method of all is to submit all of your parameters to me through my website www.darkstarBlackjack.com and I will send back a betting strategy along with all of the details on what to expect. This will include your exact risk of ruin, hourly win rate and standard deviations along with a layman's explanation of what all that means.

Trip Bankroll

So that is your Blackjack Bankroll but how much do you bring on any individual trip. If you are making your living playing Blackjack and have determined that your bankroll needs to be $35,000, you're not going to travel with the entire $35,000 in cash. You'll need to determine how much you need for any individual trip. The software will help you do this. Since a loss of greater than 2 standard deviations from the normal gain is very unlikely, that is what I recommend bringing. Just enter the number of hours you'll be playing and the rules, penetration, etc. that you expect to experience and it will predict the possible results. The program will actually go out 3 standard deviations which covers 99% of all possible outcomes.

When you get to the first table you need to be prudent in how much you buy in for. Remember, you can always buy more chips any time you need them. You will want to have enough chips to increase your bet but you want as little attention from casino bosses and surveillance as possible. I usually buy in for 3 or 4 large bets. If my maximum bet is going to be $100, I won't buy in for more than $400. This will usually insure I have enough in front of me to get out the big bets when needed without looking silly by throwing $1,000 down and then opening up with a $10 bet.

1. http://wizardofodds.com/gambling/kelly-criterion/

♦Chapter 7 - The Fine Art of Camouflage

I've been playing all night and I am winning. I'm up at least three grand. My bets are fluctuating wildly, coinciding with a card count that is jumping up and down enough to cause me whiplash. But I am up, and I have been making some very bold bets with big payoffs that are surely drawing heat.

Now, not too far off, on the other side of the pit, I hear the tiny tinkling sound of the little touch- tone phone ringing. It is the eye-in-the-sky calling the pit boss. The pit boss picks up the phone and places it to her ear. She slowly turns to look at my table. She is looking right at me! Holy Crap, this is it. I've been outed! She's is talking to whomever upstairs in a very soft voice, so as not to be heard. I'm starting to sweat now. SHIT! I just got twenty-one twice after splitting. The pit boss seems to recognize this. She is watching my game play. Now the dealer is paying me off and seems to be very showy about doing it, as if to say, "Hey Pit Boss, are you seeing this?" My stomach starts to ache. The pit boss's conversation seems to be getting louder now. As if she's saying, "Okay, we got him. Assemble the team, get down here fast and let's surround the table."

Oh my God! I've got to cash out and bolt from the casino before she gets off that phone and ID's me! She just hung up the phone and is walking straight to my table. Forget cashing out! Grab your chips and get the hell outta here!"

I have learned a lot from working on the inside of a casino. I know what they are looking for. I know who they are looking for. I know what will make the eye-in-the-sky cameras notice you. I've read all of the expert opinions in other books and so I will start off this Chapter by saying that they all got it wrong.

Let's start off by defining what we mean when we're talking about "heat" and "camouflage."

"Heat" refers to any time casino Pit Bosses or casino security are starting to watch your game play. You could say that things are getting hot if you have just been winning a lot of hands and suddenly a pit boss comes over and starts to watch your game play to the point of staring at your moves and watching no one else at the table.

"Camouflage" is the means you employ to disguise your game play so that you don't stand-out or shine like a card-counter. Camouflage can mean disguising your bets so that radical swings are not visible, or it can be as simple as pretending to drink a beer when you are trying to keep a sober head while playing. It can also be something like carrying on a conversation with a Pit Boss who is purposely trying to distract you, because he/she doesn't believe it's possible to talk and keep the count at the same time.

Perspective

If you live in the United States, you might not understand how anyone could think that bugs are delicious. Personally I think lobster is delicious despite the fact that it's basically a giant bug. But, my point is, we all have a cultural bias. Making holes in your ears to wear earrings is accepted in our culture. However, making a giant hole in your nose to wear a bone seems strange or foreign to us. Casino employees live in a different world than the rest of us.

From their point of view, the casino is offering entertainment. You are supposed to lose because that is the cost of entertainment. You are expected to drink, laugh and have a good time while playing games in the casino. You are not supposed to take this seriously and use your brain to make money. That is what the house is supposed to do.

As a professional player, I think that the casino is offering a game that only very skilled players can beat. I should be allowed and even congratulated if I can play a game they created without breaking any rules and win. I should be congratulated even if this win was due to skill and not luck. Basically, in my humble opinion, the casino is a sore loser.

What I know now

What I have learned while working on the other side of the table, is that I was often overly paranoid that I was attracting heat, when the reality was, I was usually never on the radar. A lot of Professional Blackjack players are worried that they are being watched, and they are worried about being caught and kicked out of the casino, and much worse, getting banned from the casino.

Truth be told, I have never been thrown out of a casino or even asked to leave. That may be because I usually leave on my own after the first warning. The casino would prefer you leave on your own and will most likely do something to indicate that they are on to you. I have been told that the dealer will be instructed to shuffle after every single hand until I stop counting cards and in some cases they even asked me politely not to play Blackjack anymore. In one such case, I played another game for a while at an attempt to convince them I was not a real threat. I went back to that same casino a couple of years later and played without incident.

There is one casino that I frequent that will shuffle the cards whenever I attempt "back-counting." "Back-counting" is also referred to as "Wonging-in" to a table. The technique is named after Stanford Wong who invented the technique. "Back-counting is when you are watching the shoe being dealt from the very beginning, following the shuffle, and keeping the count of all the cards being dealt, and then jumping into the middle of the shoe when the count becomes favorable.

What you have to realize, and remind yourself is, that card-counting is not illegal. Annoying to the casino? Yes. Something that the police will be called for? Absolutely not. Think of card-counting as an inconvenience for the casino. If it's obvious that you are doing it, and winning, then you are a pest.

We all get paranoid when that phone starts ringing. Well, now that I have worked on the other side, let me tell you what that's all about. That phone in the pit rings all the damn time. If you notice that the phone starts ringing, and then a floor manager and two pit bosses are huddled up and talking in hushed tones, and the phone rings again, and one of the pit bosses answers...chances are, instead of talking about you, they are trying to figure out who is going to deal Blackjack, because two employees just called in sick. They are not discussing whether they should get the Doberman Security Dogs or the Taser Gun for you. What they are likely talking about is who will be in charge of the Blackjack tournament later tonight, and which dealers will be working those tables. So, just chill out!

There are a lot of reasons why that phone in the pit rings, and very rarely is it about a particular player. In general, the only time security will call the pit, is when they see an obvious mistake by a dealer.

Surveillance is watching a lot of things. They are not just watching Blackjack. They are watching the Slot Machines, the Craps tables, the Poker tables, the Big-Spin wheel, Bingo rooms, employee break rooms, parking lots, hotel hallways, etc. To learn more about Las Vegas casino security and the NORA system (Non-Obvious Relationship Awareness) and a Blackjack-specific-technology called TableEye21, check out our blog post: Las Vegas Casino Surveillance: It's About Security, It's About Marketing, It's About Everywhere

Another thing I have learned from working both sides of the table, is that there are a lot of people who think that they know how to count cards, but don't. Also, there are people who do know how to count cards, but don't have a clue what to do with the information. It's a lot like knowing how a plane flies but not knowing how to fly a plane. So what? That's useless to me and the other passengers if we're crashing.

Casinos make a lot of money from these pseudo-professionals. Just because you know how to count-cards and just because you look like you know what you are doing, doesn't mean the pit boss will stop you right away. They are likely going to watch you for a while to see just how good you are. The last thing the casino wants to do is turn away some tool who thinks he can count, but really can't. They are likely going to make more money from him, than they can from the average player.

Let's say that you are playing at a $5 table, and that your bets are anywhere from $5 to $150. Well then you, my friend, are one big snore to security, and it's my opinion that nobody is watching you at all, because they have people betting thousands of dollars in several different areas of the casino. They are not really paying attention to the $5 and $10 tables. Even if they think you are counting, they may not be interested. Well, most of the time anyway.

Once, in a downtown Vegas casino, I was very rudely "flat-betted" while playing low stakes. Here is the situation. I was in a small Fremont Street casino at around 4 AM. They had an amazing double-deck game there. Five dollar minimum, five-thousand max and double-down on anything, double after split, and Blackjack paid the full 3:2. I just wanted to make a few extra bucks before going to bed so I thought if I bet small, I should be able to forget camouflage for an hour or so.

My max bet was only $75 but I would bet the $5 minimum whenever the count was below 1 and $75 anytime it was above 2. Looking back, it looked ridiculously obvious. I played for about 30 minutes and didn't notice any heat. The place was pretty dead though. With less than a dozen table games players in the entire joint, I should have figured they were watching me at least a little. Then came my opportunity.--all small cards for the first 2 rounds. I bet $5 on both of those and lost both. Now the count was right about +2. I bet $75 and got Blackjack. The only other player was dealt two tens. This reduced the count back below 2. So I bet $5 and lost but the round increased the count back above +2. I bet $75 again, got a pair of eights and split. Both eights produced double-downs and the double-downs produced 19 and 21. The dealer busted with something like 7, 9, Jack. The count was reduced by all of this, so I bet $5 and lost. Now, since we had less than a deck left, the true count was at least 5. I was so focused on the count and oblivious to any heat that I actually wanted to reduce my stack of red chips. I carefully counted out 15 of them and was about to slide them into the circle, when the floor manager stopped the dealer and told him to shuffle up.

They have amazing penetration at this place and we should have had a couple more hands. There was only one other player at the table and he was playing a never-bust strategy (see glossary). So we didn't use that many cards except for my eight split. After telling the dealer to shuffle up, he got right in my face and shouted, "That WAS a great count, wasn't it!".

Of course I said, "I don't know what you're talking about."

"You know exactly what I'm talking about. You're fucking counting and you don't even have the decency to try to hide it."

"I don't know how to count cards", I laughed.

"I wish you didn't because then I wouldn't have to flat-bet you. From now on, you bet $5 a hand, every hand, or you can get the fuck out!"

I was not scared despite the fact that this was the first and only time a casino employee swore at me. I was pissed. My first thought was that I was only up a few hundred and not breaking any laws. I did not immediately leave the table. Instead, I bet $5 as instructed. The other player asked me, or maybe he was asking the dealer, "What the hell was that about?" The dealer shrugged and I responded, "I guess they only want losers in here."

I still can't believe how unprofessional this supervisor was. He did this right at the table in front of another player. He had no concern for what the other player might have thought about all of this and said nothing to him. He offered no explanation for shuffling the cards early and no apology for disturbing his game.

I definitely think this was the exception, not the rule and the proof of that is what happened eight hours later. I played a couple more hands at table minimum and ordered a drink. When my drink came, I colored up, cashed out and went to my room. I was staying at this very casino. I got up that afternoon and returned to the exact same table. This time I played with a reasonable amount of camouflage -- no raise after a push and no bet increases greater than double the last bet. I played this way for at least three hours at the same table and no one said a word to me. This meant that I was not put on any kind of watch list and he probably didn't even mention it to the floor manager that relieved him. If he did, he either didn't show my picture to the new floor manager, or maybe the day shift manager thought he over-reacted and ignored the information.

What you need to get out of this long story is that this was the worst that ever happened to me. He swore at me and "flat-betted" me. He didn't have a couple of security goons beat me up in the back room and he didn't even kick me out. I've seen card-counters escorted out. In those instances they were very polite and more discrete than this joker. Also, it's important to remain calm. I was very angry but had I shouted back or made an even bigger scene, I doubt I would have been able to play there on the next shift. I may even have had to look for a new hotel room at four in the morning.

Tactics

If you're going to play Blackjack for a living and this is going to be your business, I would recommend that you start off by being as anonymous as possible. So, when they ask you to sign up for a player's card, which they will do often and every time you play, I would politely decline. I wouldn't want them to know who I am. I don't want them to know my real name.

I'm not interested in getting rated. I'm not interested in getting comps like free hotel rooms, free meals, free drinks, etc.

However, if you're playing for fun, maybe you do want the perks that go along with frequent casino play. It's up to you to decide.

Sometimes the floor managers can be really pushy with the loyalty cards, so I tell them, "No thanks, because when I get those cards, it just makes me want to gamble more. I already gamble more than I should, so I am just better off without it. I end up playing too long just to earn points.

Just so you know, in a small casino, like some of the many tiny Native-American casinos around the country, it is impossible to stay anonymous. One that I frequent only has 4 Blackjack tables, and sometimes only 1 table is open! Plus, they only have Blackjack for about 12 hours a day, so you see the same dealers all of the time. There is no way they are not going to know who I am. I can tell them I don't want to get a card, but at some point, I am going to have to tell them a name, even if it's a fake name. Maybe they will know me as Moses, but the fact that I don't have a card and that I've given them a fake name, is not going to stop them from throwing me out. So, in those places, you might as well tell them your real name.

Some pros will choose to disguise their appearance in whatever way they can get away with. For example, they may wear a hat and hang their head down to hide their face a little bit. This can go a long way to hiding your identity because the cameras are positioned up high. Some casinos will ask you to remove your hat. If you're asked, you're better off removing it immediately because you will only draw more attention to yourself if you refuse to remove it. If you know the casino has a no hat policy, then leave your hat in the car.

Most casinos will not let you wear sunglasses at the table, so, that's out as a disguise.

Before I became a dealer, I used to try and make it look like I was losing. However, now that I have insider knowledge, I don't do this anymore. It's the floor managers job to keep track of how much money everybody has. Even when I've tried to sneak a few black chips in my pocket, the floor managers notice that right away.

I don't claim to be perfect. This book is about helping you learn from my mistakes. One time, at a small casino where I am known very well, I pretended to lose and made a fool of myself. Only a card-counter can make a fool of himself by winning and acting like a loser. I played for a good eight hours at one table with no other players the entire time. This is a dream scenario because it was double-deck with great rules and even better penetration.

I knew I was winning and I was using minimal camouflage. I started discretely sliding black and purple chips into my pocket. I figured I was up about $5,500 and was tired and hungry. I slid the chips in front of me toward the dealer and said, "I think I lost enough for one day." The Pit Boss heard this and exclaimed, "Lost? I haven't seen anyone win that much in a long time! Wish I could lose like that!"

What a loser! I didn't work in a casino at the time but should have realized that the casino is keeping track of how much money the table is up or down at all times. I was the only player and the table was down $7,500. Oh yeah! By the way, as I was stashing those purple and blacks away, four purples ended up in my coat pocket rather than my pants like the others. It wasn't until I got home that I realized I was actually up $7,500. I'm lucky no one stole my coat as it lie unattended across a Burger King chair with $2,000 worth of casino chips in the outside pocket, while I used the restroom.

Sleight of Hand

Another technique is, disguising the amount of my bet increase. Let's say my last bet was $25 but the count is telling me I should really bet $100 now, so rather than just taking the bet I won and staking it up to make $50, I covertly grab 2 quarters and palm them, grab the 2 quarters in the circle between my fingertips and then let the whole stack of 4 quarters fall on my betting stack. To the casual observer, it looks like I'm just stacking it up, but in fact I have a $100 bet. This won't fool the Eye-in-the-sky but they may not be watching. The floor manager and dealer would have to be watching you carefully to notice. They will certainly see that the bet is now $100 but will probably just think it must have been $50 last time. I wouldn't try it if you are the only player at the table or if there is only one other guy and he's betting table minimum every hand. Getting caught using camouflage is worse than not using camouflage at all.

Please don't confuse this with capping my bet, after the fact, which is illegal. This is before the dealer closes betting and then begins dealing.

Feign Emotion

If you really are losing, use this as an opportunity to make use of free camouflage. Most gamblers get upset when they lose. Most card-counters do not. Hopefully, you will not truly be upset but act like you are.

Wonging In

Stanford Wong is one of the fathers of card-counting and invented a system of back-counting or "Wonging" where you are standing behind or next to the table and watch a shoe of cards being dealt. You keep track of the count of all cards hitting the table. Then, whenever the count gets to an optimal point, you jump into the game and start betting.

A lot of pros employ this method, but you have to be careful how you implement this. A DarkStar master will make it look like he/she is looking at the table as an after-thought, rather than standing directly behind and staring at the table. I have been caught a couple of times doing this, and a teammate and friend of mine got busted, thrown out and banned from a casino because he was being ridiculously obvious.

This is how I prefer to do it: I pretend to be watching a neighboring table. If no cards are being dealt, there is no reason to be looking at that table. As you get better and better at card- counting, you will get to a point where you can look at a table strewn with cards and instantly know the count. This comes with time.

"Wonging" or back-counting is not typically used as camouflage. The purpose is to not bet at all unless the count is in your favor. However, it can be a type of camouflage because if done correctly, it looks better than jumping your bet from $10 to $500 or even $10 to $100. If you are using it as camouflage, be smart about when you jump in.

Many players will watch tables before playing. Most of them are not card-counters. Most are watching to see how the other players play because they believe in the myth that if everyone at the table plays "right", the whole table will win more often. Also, many players believe in the "change the cards" myth. If the count gets to the point where you want to get in (maybe around +2) wait till at least one player loses before sitting down.

Waiting till someone loses or everyone loses may cost you the opportunity to get in or at least miss a good round or two. That is the cost of camouflage. You need to understand that camouflage is an expense. You will make more money if you don't use any camouflage at all but you might also be shown the door.

Ice-Cream Camouflage

I may have invented this an an excuse to eat ice cream. A definite possibility since I thought of it while playing in a casino that serves Cashew Cherry in a waffle cone and you can walk around the casino with it. You cannot, however, play Blackjack while eating anything. Most casinos have this rule and you can use it to your advantage.

I walk around back-counting tables while I eat my ice cream cone. When I find a good count, I toss the cone or inhale it. Careful the freeze headache doesn't make you lose the count. Quickly grab a seat and buy in. If the count is negative, I don't have to worry about dealers or floor managers encouraging me to play. I have the perfect excuse and they won't even try to get me to play. Last thing they want to do is clean up an ice cream spill on the felt.

Seat Selection

The best place to sit is third base. Sometimes called the anchor, it is the spot furthest to the dealer's right. You will be the last one to make a decision on your hand and will see more cards before you make that decision than anyone else. Casino surveillance and supervisors know that card-counters prefer that spot. Additionally, you will get more attention from the other players when you are in that spot. They will call attention to what they think are smart plays and vise-versus, especially when you take or leave a card that affects the outcome for the dealer's hand. i.e. you stand on 16 against the dealer's 10 and the dealer flips a 6 for the hole-card and draws a 4. Now some of the players are blaming you because you could have had 20 instead of the dealer. The only reason you should care is that you want as little attention as possible if you are to remain incognito. This is why I only sit at third base when it is the only available seat.

Bigger is Better

Figure 1 Do you think this man is admiring her belt?

This may sound silly, but there are pros who bring their wives or girlfriends, if they are well endowed or hire an escort model to sit at the table with them or to stand directly behind the table. Do you think the eye-in-the-sky guy (most are males) is really watching your game play or do you thinks he's zoomed in on those breasts? Guess. Think about it. These are guys like any other guys who have a very boring job of watching everything under the sun..what do you think they want to be looking at?

Drinking

Casinos want you to drink because it fucks up your game. I'm sorry but there is no nice way to say this that conveys the necessary urgency that, under no circumstances, should you be drinking alcohol while playing Blackjack. It's a recipe for losing money. Many times I have been offered a free drink to the point where the pit boss is insisting. When this happens, I will order a beer that comes in a dark bottle or a can so that he can't see me NOT drinking the beer he bought for me. I will pretend to take sips and eventually leave the table and go to the restroom and dump the beer in a trash can on my way. Another method is to enter the table with soda and lime and sip that for the duration. When the pit boss offers to buy another round of what he guesses is an alcoholic drink, you can tell him, "No thanks, I've had enough. Just regular soda for me from here on out."

An amusing thing happened one time. I did get caught doing this. I left my beer at the table while on a restroom break. This was the beer that I was supposedly drinking over the course of an hour. It was still full despite the fact that I had put it up to my lips over a dozen times. On my way back to the table, I had to make some phone calls. The floor manager picked up the beer and tracked me down in the middle of the casino, nowhere near the table and said, "I was going to throw this out but realized it's still full, do you still want this?"
So, in that situation, it was obvious that he knew I was faking drinking the beer. It would have been better had I just declined the beer in the first place. Awkward!

Interestingly, that particular floor manager, several months later, called me out as a card-counter, and he went so far as to identify which betting system I was using and how I was using it. However, he let me keep playing and he's done nothing to keep me from going back.

When and How Much Camouflage to Use

How much camouflage to use is ultimately up to you and it depends on who you are as well. The TSA is not supposed to use racial profiling but we all know they are more suspicious of Middle Eastern passengers than others. The same is true, if not more so, for casino surveillance and management. If you are a woman, I would use very little camouflage at all. Just don't dress like a tom-boy. If you look like you just graduated from MIT with a computer science degree you will need more camouflage than a woman wearing a peek-a-boo blouse.

Which one is the Card-counter?

Intentional Play Errors

Anytime you deviate either from Basic Strategy or from an Illustrious 18 play when the true count or index number calls for it, you are costing yourself money. The cost of that error is less than the amount of your bet and is a cost even if you end up winning the hand. I cover that in more detail in the chapter on running a Blackjack business. If you plan to play Blackjack for a living, it is a necessary cost of doing business. There are some play decisions that make you look more like a card-counter than others.

In the past, I used to split 10s, but I no longer do that. So, if you have a high count of +6 or higher, and the dealer has a 5 or 6 showing, mathematically it makes sense to split your 10s in that situation. I won't do it because there are only two people that split 10s-- card-counters and morons. Now, if you have clearly demonstrated, up to this point, that you are not an idiot, and have been playing Blackjack pretty well. When you are faced with a pair of 10s that you have never split before and have a higher than average bet out there, we'll say $150, so you throw another $150 and split those 10s. What do you think the casino will think when they see this? Either you've suddenly and completely lost your mind, or you have just revealed yourself in a super-obvious way as a card-counter. If you make this move, the casino will know right away that you are a card-counter. You would have to play your Columbo routine pretty convincingly and have them thinking you are a bumbling idiot in order to pull this one over on them.

The other one that comes up frequently is a hard 16 against the dealer's 10. I always stand on this hand. The reason is that anytime the count is positive I will want to stand and when the count is negative I will have my minimum bet out there. So the cost of this error is very low. In fact, it's the lowest cost error you can make. It's cheap and effective camouflage. Doing this against any other dealer card is not advisable because then the cost goes up significantly.

Other than splitting tens, the easiest way to get identified as a card-counter is by taking insurance when you have a stiff hand. Especially if the dealer actually has Blackjack and you end up pushing with 15. Because it's called insurance and most players buy in to the false pretense that they are insuring their hand, many people will insure a hand like 20 or take even money (same as insurance) on a Blackjack. Insuring a 13 seems ludicrous to them and you will likely get comments when you do it. However, you know that when the true count is +3 or more, the likelihood of a ten hiding under the dealer's Ace is high enough to make the insurance bet profitable in the long run. To counter this you could spend some money on insurance when you have a small bet and a twenty. If the casino thinks you are counting but making mistakes, they will likely let you play.

What about betting more than double the previous bet? I occasionally will do that depending on where I am playing, how well they know me and how much heat I think I'm going to get. Have I ever been stopped there for counting before? You want to use your best judgment the first time and see how much attention you get. You'll have a feeling for it. In places where they know me as a regular gambler, I tend to do some crazy things. By crazy I mean betting and playing according to the count even if it looks crazy to the average player. In a place where I haven't been before, my game play is more conservative.

In Las Vegas, their antennae is more attuned to detecting card-counters than casinos in the Midwest.

I never raise after a push. Very few players will raise after a push, so if I get a push and the count goes up, I won't raise my bet. I just leave it out there. Likewise, if the count declines.

Title 31

Years back the US Bank Secrecy Act (also known as Title 31) was created to focus on financial institutions that might be involved in money laundering. However, as the nation (yes, the IRS) got more involved in tracking the flow of large currency transactions, the casino industry got swept into the act and now must also report certain currency transactions to the Financial Crimes Enforcement Network, known as FinCEN, of the IRS.

(cashing in chips, TITO's, cash for bank documents, money orders etc.). At a threshold of $3,000 the casino is required to produce an MTL (Multiple transaction log) that details the player's description, player account number, social security number if on file, and the time of any transactions.

That cash transaction level is not the one that people fear. The one that catches people off-guard is what is called a CTRC, or Currency transaction report-casino, that must be produced should a player cross the threshold of $10,000 in cash transactions in a single 24-hour gaming period. When this happens, the casino is required to obtain the player's name, current address, legal ID, and social security number.

There is some leeway on the social, as a player can fill out a W-9 form that simply lists their social security number, an actual social security card is not required. However, the number will be checked by the casino and if it does not match the name and ID given, the player will not be allowed to gamble in the future. And, if the ID provided is not current (if it is expired), the player will not be allowed to continue gaming and must leave the premises. Additionally the casino is required to deny the transaction. Meaning you will be able to get cash for your chips if you refuse ID or do not have proper ID.

It does not matter how much you are winning or losing at any time in the casino. The only requirement is that you have gone over the $10,000 cash limit in a 24-hour gaming period. And, the casino can not give you a "heads-up" that you are approaching the $10,000 limit. In fact, once you pull the cash out of your pocket and try to buy chips, if the transaction will put you over $10,000 the requirements have been met for the casino to produce a CTRC. You can't just take some of the cash back and act like it didn't happen, and neither can the casino, so don't try and make a deal. The casino can be heavily fined, and so can the Pit boss or manager who is involved, if the paperwork is not completed.

It is illegal for any casino employee to help a player circumvent any aspects of Title 31, including not reporting or under-reporting any cash transactions, or giving out information about a casino's 24-hour gaming day. [1]

Any transaction that is over $3,000 can be considered suspicious activity under the right circumstances. For that reason, I don't ever cash-out for more than $1,500 at a time. And, you can't just go from one window and get $1,500 and go to another window and get $1,500, and so on, because that can be considered "structuring" which will get you in even more hot water.

The Bottom Line on Camouflage

Don't worry about it too much. You can start worrying about it when you get thrown out of a casino. You're not going to get "back-roomed" like they show in the movies. No one is going to beat you up.

1.http://casinogambling.about.com/od/casinoterms/a/Title-31-And-Casino-Gambling.htm

♠ Chapter 8 -Team Play

First let me say I am not a big proponent of Blackjack teams. I think they are more trouble than they are worth and have the potential of creating problems you don't need. Most of what you saw in the movie "21" was bullshit, but it is still a good example of problems that can occur with a team. Now that I got that off my chest, I will describe a few ways to set up a team because I said this was a complete book on Blackjack and many Blackjack teams have existed and continue to exist.

There are several ways to set up a Blackjack team. If you saw the movie "21", you think you know what team play is. For those who did not see the movie, I'll give a brief explanation. Most of the team members make minimum wager bets and keep the running count. They play Basic Strategy without variations. Let's call them Spotters because they are looking for a table with a good count. If the table gets so negative that it will likely not improve with enough cards left to make money, they move on. However, if the count gets above a predetermined entry point, the Spotter would signal the Big Player. The Big Player would buy into the table with a large amount of cash. The amount depends on your bankroll but you will need a very large bankroll to make this a profitable venture. The Spotter would covertly pass the running count to the Big Player. In the movie they used a code. Different words represented different numbers. "Sweet", for example, meant 16. They would use it in a sentence like, "this coffee is too sweet." The Big Player would convert the running count to the true count and make very large bets. He would play Basic Strategy with the variations I explained earlier. The Spotter would stay at the table and continue to make minimum wager bets and play Basic Strategy. She would also keep counting. The Big Player would make very large wagers and play until the count got to zero or less. Then he would color up his chips and find a new table.

This method of team play is basically very expensive camouflage. The purpose is to allow the Big Player to make large bets when the odds favor the player and bet nothing at all when it favors the house. Since the Spotters are making minimum wager bets all of the time, it works out to the same profit margin as the Big Player making minimum wager bets when the count is low and large bets when the count is high. Since that would draw too much attention and get the Big Player removed from the casino and possibly barred from playing, the Spotters are used as camouflage. This is truly the way the MIT teams play.

I don't know the exact amounts that they work with but the Spotters bet between $15 and $25 depending on the tables they can find and the Big Player bets at least $1,000 per hand. You can see that an individual betting $25 most of the time and then suddenly betting $1,000 or more would look suspicious. In order to pull this off you would need to buy in for several thousand dollars and then proceed to bet $25 or buy in again despite having chips in front of you, in order to start making four figure bets. The dealer would definitely need approval from a floor manager for a large buy in and at that level post 9-11, they will want ID etc. So you go through all of that when you get to the table and then bet minimum for the first three rounds or more. Say the count never gets to +2. Now you walk away with $10,000 in chips, having wagered only $100 or so. Guess what? You just got an SAR report filed in your name with the IRS, FBI and Department of Homeland Security not to mention casino management, security and surveillance. What if the count does improve? Now you suddenly jump your bet from $25 to $1,500 and continue to bet over $1,000 per round until the count drops back down and you either leave or go back to minimum. Would you not say, "What the Hell was that?" if you were the dealer?

Let's take a look at how this would work in reality. How much money would you need to employ this method and how many Spotters would you need? First, you are going to have to play at large corporate casinos where they have tables with a minimum of $25 and a max of $5,000. In addition to the money the Spotters are expected to lose at the table, you will have to pay them something. By now you should know that the method of play the Spotters are using is a losing proposition. In the movie they got a share of the profits, assuming there were some. In the movie they had three Spotters and one Big Player. So we'll use that for our simulation. Also we'll use typical Las Vegas Strip rules since that is where they played in the movie. That means Dealer Hits Soft 17, Double-Down on any two cards, Split Aces Once, No action after Ace Split, Split any other pair 3 times, Double after Split, No Surrender and Blackjack pays 3:2. Cards are dealt out of a six deck shoe. Penetration is about 4 ½ out of 6 or 75%. The Big Player enters at +2 and leaves at +1. We want the Big Player's risk-of-ruin to be 1% or less.

250,000,000 Round Simulation

I ran the simulation with 250 million rounds of Blackjack and here is what it looks like. You would need a bankroll of $250,000 plus expenses. The Spotters would bet $25 no matter what the count was. The Big Player would bet $1,000 at a true count of 1 or 2, $1250 at 3 and $1500 at 4 or more. The Big Player would average $212 per hour and the Spotters would lose an average of $11 times 3 Spotters or $33 an hour. So $212 - $33 = $179 per hour on average. I always look at 2 standard deviations from the average on both sides of the bell curve to cover what will happen 95% of the time. You will almost never hit the average on the head. So the Big Player will have results between a loss of $3948 and a win of $4372 per hour.

To figure out the business plan, you would use the average of $179 per hour. If you split that equally between the four team members, everyone would earn an average of $44.75 an hour. However, you would want to run this like a business. Therefore you would want to take some of the profit and cover expenses and add to the bankroll in case you had a losing trip. The percent you add back to the business is up to you of course but I would put at least 25% back into the business to cover expenses and grow the bankroll. That means only $33.56 an hour. Still an okay living but the camouflage is costing you and the business $133.68 an hour! There has to be a better way!

A Better Way

I told you that I made a lot of mistakes when I first started. Early on Enoch and I tried the team play method described above. We didn't have any fancy software at that time so we relied on his math skills to develop the betting strategy. Enoch was the Big Player and myself and two others were Spotters. Even when we won big, it seemed like we had very little left after paying expenses. It was an okay way for four friends to have a good time at the expense of the casino but we were trying to make a living.

I suggested that the Spotters not play. They could simply back-count and signal the Big Player when the count got to +1 or better. When the Big Player approached the table he could simply walk past the Spotter who would tell him the count. The way we did it was the Spotter would take out his cell phone as the signal to enter the table. Then when the Big Player walked past, the Spotter would just say the count. No code needed because it would just seem like he or she was talking on the phone.

Of course we didn't have a quarter million dollar bankroll. Even if we did, this modification only saves $33 an hour. Your still have to pay the

Spotters something. We realized that we could easily do it with 2 Spotters and 2 Big Players. Now, if you had that quarter million bankroll, you could make $424 per hour. If you took 25% off the top to go back into the business you would have $318 per hour to split however you saw fit amongst the four of you. You could even let the Spotters play and get up when the count got high as the signal. That would only cost you $22 an hour while they played. I would have done the first example that way but wanted to make the point that you can't always believe what you see in the movies or on TV. There are plenty of people that saw the movie and thought they could recreate it. Proof that a little knowledge can be more dangerous than no knowledge at all.

Men are Pigs

This method works best if the Big Player is a man and the Spotter is a woman but two women could also pull it off. This is not for everyone but could be a lot of fun for some. Usually the purpose of team play is to avoid being seen as a professional player and getting barred from the casino.

The Spotter will be playing in this strategy. She will typically wear a very revealing top. Since the important thing is how she looks while seated at the table, the length of the skirt is not important. Think about the position of the cameras sometimes referred to as the eye-in-the-sky. The two of you come to the table at the beginning of the shoe. Pick a table with no players or as few players as possible. The lady buys in for a couple hundred and makes minimum bets. She plays Basic Strategy. The man or other woman does not play and either sits next to her or stands behind her. Some casinos will not let you sit at the table if you are not playing. If they have this rule but ignore it when you sit down, you'll know it's working. If possible, I would choose a table with a male dealer. The dealer is not the one you should worry about but he might be inclined to ignore the play to sit rule if he's afraid his eye candy will leave with you.

It's important that both of you keep the count. When and if the true count reaches +2, the Spotter will say something like, "Aren't you going to play, Honey?" The Big Player will then buy in and make large bets until the count drops below plus one or wherever you decide. No one will likely pay attention to the count because they will either be looking at your girlfriend or watching another table because she's only playing minimum. When you buy in for a few thousand it will just look like you are showing off. You can even sit out a few hands when the count drops and let her play and jump back in. Don't vary your bets much. You'll want to keep a tight range or you'll be pushing your luck with surveillance. I'm not going to go through the math on this one. If you want to try it you can submit to me at www.darkstarBlackjack.com.

Another Reason for a Team

At this point you might be thinking the team approach only works if you have a six figure bankroll. If you're using a team to avoid casino heat, that's true. If you have a more modest bankroll, you'll be less of a threat to the casino and will have less need for camouflage. Two or more skilled players could also set up a team in order to combine bankrolls. It's important for there to be mutual trust and respect with any team but it is of paramount importance in this scenario. You will definitely want to play at different tables and arrive separately. Even avoid playing the same casino on the same day if possible. So you can see how you will need to have complete trust in the other team member or members. Many teams have used polygraphs to keep people honest.

♡ Chapter 9 - Progressive Betting

There are a lot of books on Blackjack and they typically fall into two major categories: Books about Card Counting systems and books about Progressive Betting systems. The obvious question is which one is better? Let's examine the facts to see if we can answer this question.

Progressive Betting is a system designed to take advantage of "runs" or "streaks" to maximize wins and minimize losses. Many gamblers believe that winning and losing goes in streaks. It is curious why does the progressive bettor choose to play Blackjack? Winning and losing streaks are not unique to Blackjack, perhaps because Blackjack has the lowest house advantage of any game in the casino.

Since Progressive Betting is based on the notion of streaks, let's examine "streaks" more carefully.

Are Streaks Real?

Consider a study conducted by the University of Rochester funded by the National Science Foundation and Behavior Research Foundation to Hayden that reveals that even monkeys share in our unfounded beliefs in winning and losing streaks. According to the study:

"The results suggests that the penchant to see patterns that actually don't exist... The cognitive bias may be difficult to override

even in situations that are truly random. This inborn tendency to feel that we are on a roll or in a slump may help explain why

gambling can be so alluring and why the stock market is so prone to wild swings... The monkeys showed the hot-hand bias

consistently over weeks of play and an average of 1,244 trials per condition. "They had lots and lots of opportunities to get

over this bias, to learn and change, and yet they continued to show the same tendency."

So why do monkeys and humans share this false belief in a run of luck even when faced over and over with evidence that the results are random? The authors speculate that the distribution of food in the wild, which is not random, may be the culprit. "If you find a nice juicy beetle on the underside of a log, this is pretty good evidence that there might be a beetle in a similar location nearby, because beetles, like most food sources, tend to live near each other," explained coauthor Benjamin Hayden, assistant professor brain and cognitive sciences at the University of Rochester.

Evolution has also primed our brains to look for patterns, added Hayden. "We have this incredible drive to see patterns in the world, and we also have this incredible drive to learn. I think it's very related to why we like music, and why we like to do crossword puzzles, Sudoku, and things like that. If there's a pattern there, we're on top of it. And if there may or may not be a pattern there, that's even more interesting." [1.]

Maybe a study on monkeys is not going to convince you. After all you've probably experienced a run of good or bad luck more than once. I'm not saying we don't occasionally see a run of several wins or losses in a row. I'm simply saying that the reason we remember them is that they are the exception not the rule. Humans have selective memory bias-- a cognitive bias that either enhances or impairs the recall of a memory or that alters the content of a reported memory. For example, if you have a hypothesis about anything, you will remember events that support your theory and tend to forget or ignore the ones that disprove it. I once won or pushed (tied) every hand in a six deck shoe. I have also lost every hand. In literally decades of playing Blackjack, sometimes 6 days a week, each of these events happened only once.

Gambler's Fallacy

The gambler's fallacy can be illustrated by considering the repeated toss of a fair coin. With a fair coin, the outcomes in different tosses are statistically independent and the probability of getting heads on a single toss is exactly ½ (one in two). It follows that the probability of getting two heads in two tosses is $\frac{1}{4}$ (one in four) and the probability of getting three heads in three tosses is $\frac{1}{8}$ (one in eight). In general, if we let A_i be the event that toss i of a fair coin comes up heads, then we have,

$$\Pr\left(\bigcap_{i=1}^{n} A_i\right) = \prod_{i=1}^{n} \Pr(A_i) = \frac{1}{2^n}.$$

Now suppose that we have just tossed four heads in a row, so that if the next coin toss were also to come up heads, it would complete a run of five successive heads. Since the probability of a run of five successive heads is only $\frac{1}{32}$ (one in thirty-two), a person subject to the gambler's fallacy might believe that this next flip was less likely to be heads than to be tails. However, this is not correct, and is a manifestation of the gambler's fallacy; the event of 5 heads in a row and the event of "first 4 heads, then a tails" are equally likely, each having probability $\frac{1}{32}$. Given that the first four rolls turn up heads, the probability that the next toss is a head is in fact,

$$\Pr\left(A_5 | A_1 \cap A_2 \cap A_3 \cap A_4\right) = \Pr\left(A_5\right) = \frac{1}{2}.$$

While a run of five heads is only $\frac{1}{32} = 0.03125$, it is only that *before* the coin is first tossed. *After* the first four tosses the results are no longer unknown, so their probabilities are 1. Reasoning that it is more likely that the next toss will be a tail than a head due to the past tosses, that a run of luck in the past somehow influences the odds in the future, is the fallacy. [2.]

Donald Dahl's Blackjack Challenge

In "Progression Blackjack" Donald Dahl issued a challenge to all card-counters. Dahl challenges any card counter to meet him at a casino and play using only a $300 bankroll. He will use the same bankroll and play his progression and the card-counter will play according to the count. He believes the card-counter will lose his bankroll first. He doubts any card counter will take him up on his challenge. He's right about that because it is not a fair fight. I would never recommend anyone attempt to beat the casino at their own game with only $300. The casino has over $300 million in their arsenal. I know of no respected professional player that would ever advise attacking a Blackjack game with less than a thousand dollars.

Donald Dahl also states that no card counter would take him up on it because all of the card-counting books require at least $1,000 bankroll. He also says about card-counters, **"Their teachings are based on a sound mathematical foundation."** [3.] I couldn't agree more, but how could he say that when he subtitled his book, "Exposing the Card Counting Myth"? I would like to know Dahl's definition of a myth. How could it be based on a sound mathematical foundation and a myth at the same time? Maybe in the bizzaro world he lives in, arithmetic, algebra and calculus are myths. I'd like to know his thoughts on gravity.

One only needs to read the back cover of his book to see that his theory makes no sense. (4)

$8.95 U. S. ($10.95 Canada)

PROGRESSION BLACKJACK

EXPOSING THE
CARD COUNTING MYTH
AND GETTING AN EDGE IN "21"

The card counting systems developed in the early 1960s gave the players a significant advantage over the casino. Over the years, the casinos have essentially eliminated this advantage through rule changes, quick shuffles and, most essential for them, multiple decks. Count systems taught today are all based on outdated strategies of the sixties.

Progression Blackjack offers a better alternative to the card counting strategy. The player need not be required to count cards, divide totals, and memorize extensive charts to gain an advantage over the house. The system outlined here teaches you to make more money on the winning hands than is lost on losing hands. This strategy minimizes possible losses and maximizes probable gains. A large bankroll is no longer required to support a viable system. Regardless of your income, with a little bit of luck, you will be more secure in making larger bets than ever before.

This book offers so revolutionary a strategy that novices will use it to master the game and veteran players will consider previous books and methods obsolete.

Donald A. Dahl regularly derives a sizable portion of his income from gambling. He has studied the game of blackjack for more than twenty years and mastered every system fabricated. Like Dr. Edward O. Thorpe, author of *Beat the Dealer*, Dahl has a strong mathematical background. He was a naval nuclear engineer for most of his working life, and his academic credentials include graduation at the top of his class at the Bettis Atomic Power Laboratory Nuclear Design School.

Cover design by Amy King

A Citadel Press Book
Carol Publishing Group

ISBN 0-8065-1396-9

50895

9 780806 513966

So let me get this straight...In order to stop card-counters, the casinos changed how they operate by making it easier for the rest of us to make money. So, anyone with a couple hundred bucks and a Basic Strategy chart can win consistently, right? No memorizing charts? No keeping track of cards dealt? Just bet more when you win, and less when you lose???That's like saying, in order to protect the country from thermonuclear weapons, we have redesigned all skyscrapers to withstand a nuclear attack. However, this design also makes it possible to destroy a building with a single shot from a Red Rider BB Gun.

He also says that while the casino can kick card-counters out and even ban them from the casino, there is nothing they can do about progressive bettors.

Why not? Both are playing according to the rules that the casino set up and both are using information available to all players. In fact, the casino will admit that card-counting is not cheating and not illegal. They have the right to prevent anyone from playing simply because of the laws governing private property. Basically, just like you can choose not to gamble with them, they can choose not to gamble with you. If the casino thought the progressive bettor was a threat, they could throw a progressive bettor out for the same reasons.

Dahl's full system is to follow Basic Strategy and his progression. Half of the equation is Basic Strategy. Most casinos will not let you have anything on the table except your chips, drink, and Basic Strategy card. Cigarette packs, lighters, and cell phones are just a few of the things that you must keep off the Blackjack table. That means the casino is more afraid of a pack of cigarettes than a Basic Strategy card.

Why do you suppose that is? Because a Basic Strategy card will only help you lose, less. A device disguised as a cigarette case might actually have a camera and mini-computer that can keep track of all the cards dealt and tell the player when to increase her bet and how to play his hand. Casinos do not remove progressive bettors, because they actually make more money from them than any other type of player, and they know that.

Both Systems Put to the Test

If you're still not convinced that progression betting is going to result in greater losses than no system at all, take a look at this experiment. Here are the results of simulation run by Blackjack-scams.com using CVData from QFIT.

Blackjack systems are tested with Blackjack simulators. An enormous number of hands are dealt following the rules of a system to see the results. For this test, I simulated four players as follows:

1.) Player 1: Flat bettor. All bets are the same.

2.) Player 2: Flat bettor that stops after four consecutive losses. This tests the belief that stop losses can affect the game.

3.) Player 3: This player uses a popular strategy found in the book *21st Century Blackjack* by Walter Thomason. Without going into details, this is basically a 2-3-4-5 positive progression, reset on shuffle, stop after four consecutive losses. But any progression will do as they are all the same.

4.) Player 4: Hi-Lo card counter spreading 1-8. I call this a lazy counter because only very simple card counting betting is utilized. No indexes are used.

5.) All players play exactly the same Basic Strategy except that the card counter bets Insurance according to the count.

6.) All players receive exactly the same cards.

7.) Total amount bet is measured including splits, insurance and double downs.

8.) One billion hands were run.

Results

	Flat Bettor	Flat - Quit Point	Progression	Lazy Counter
Total Bet	1,117,195,792	1,040,292,612	1,958,609,150	1,482,615,223
Won/Lost	-6,299,091	-5,895,908	-11,160,380	709,668
Won per $100 Bet	-$0.564	-$0.567	-$0.570	$0.048

There are only tiny differences between the flat bettor, flat bettor with quit point, and Thomason strategy from *21st Century Blackjack*. The progression strategy is a bit worse than flat betting as predicted by *Theory of Blackjack*. Of course, the counter fares far better. The counter's profit is small because playing indexes were not used. In other words, progression betting and stop losses had almost no effect on results and losses. Card counting wins.

One Billion Hands

It is oft asked what does running one billion hands matter when I won't play that many in my entire life. The point is to increase the accuracy of the estimate of what will happen in the short-term. The above numbers show that a flat bettor making 1,000 ten dollar bets will, on average, lose 60 cents less than a Thomason bettor risking the same dollars. Progression books often look at a very small number of hands, say 10,000. Well, for any 10,000 hands it is easy to come up with a system that will win. But, it will only win for that particular 10,000 hands. That doesn't mean it will win for the next 10,000 hands.

Note: Many Blackjack progression system peddlers claim that simulators are not accurate because they don't shuffle like casinos. But, the CVData Blackjack Simulator can simulate any Blackjack shuffle in excruciating detail. [5.]

Conclusion

As you can see, even for the recreational player who does not want to learn card-counting or wants to play for fun, he or she would be better off just flat betting the table minimum. That way you wouldn't have to think at all. You could use a Basic Strategy card to play your hand, drink the casino's free liquor and lose less than you would playing a progression which still involves a little concentration.

Of course, the only way to actually put the odds in your favor and make a living playing Blackjack is to learn everything I teach you here, be properly bankrolled, think when you play and most importantly, prepare and practice, practice, practice. In other words, just like anything worthwhile, it is not going to be easy. If it were as easy as the proponents of progressive betting systems make it sound, casinos would have given up on Blackjack long ago.

Blackjack currently exists in a perfect balance. Only very well trained professionals with a proper bankroll and skill set can beat the game in the long run. The casino makes enormous profits off the masses who want to try their luck, just have fun or have been fooled by a progressive betting book while DarkStar Blackjack Masters can earn a nice living. A perfect ecosystem that will keep the casino and the professional player in the black.

1..   Hot-hand bias in rhesus monkeys. Blanchard, Tommy C.; Wilke, Andreas; Hayden, Benjamin Y. Journal of Experimental Psychology: Animal Learning and Cognition, Vol 40(3), Jul 2014, 280-286.
http://dx.doi.org/10.1037/xan0000033

2.   Gambler's fallacy. Wikipedia. 05/11/15
http://en.wikipedia.org/wiki/Gambler%27s_fallacy

3.   Donald Dahl, Progression Blackjack: Exposing The
Card Counting Myth And Getting An Edge in "21" (New York:
Carol Publishing Group, 1993) 51

4.   Donald Dahl, Progression Blackjack: Exposing The
Card Counting Myth And Getting An Edge in "21" (New York:
Carol Publishing Group, 1993) back cover

5.   http://www.Blackjack-
scams.com/html/prog_systems.html

♣ Chapter 10 - Running a Blackjack Business

If you want to be a DarkStar Master and want to make a living playing Blackjack, you need to treat it as a business. You are going to have to pay your taxes and possibly pay your employees. In addition to paying yourself, you will want the business itself to be profitable. I have some experience running a business. The only major difference of this business from any other business is, that you will not have any marketing expenses. You'll want to stay as anonymous as possible. So, you'll have the opposite of marketing expense.

Since I don't know you or how much money you have or can raise for a Blackjack career, I can't tell you exactly how to run your business in this book. What I can do is help you learn from my mistakes and give you the basic framework that you'll need.

Nerves of Steal

The computer simulations prove that in the long run, you will make money if you play according to how I taught you. Those same simulations show that short term losses can be quite frequent. You need to play like a computer. If you let your emotions get the better of you, you will exacerbate the problem. There will be plenty of times when the cards seem to make no sense.

Imagine you are a DarkStar ninja, slowly and quietly making his way through the enemy's village as the guards sleep. Each step, each movement is stealthy, and carefully calculated. You are a Ninja machine!

Here's just one example. I had a pair of sevens against the dealer's seven, and the count was sky high. Without hesitation, I split the sevens and got another seven. This casino allows you to split up to three times. I split again and got a 4. Doubled and was dealt another 7. Then came a 2 on the next 7 and the count was high enough to double that. Of course since Hi-Opt I ignores 2's, I got another 2 on my 9! On the next 7, I was dealt yet another 7. Of course, I split again and ended up with 18 doubled, 11 doubled, 17 and 19.

I'm already adding it up. The count is very high but we have used more Aces than usual, so the dealer has 17 and I will win one double-down, lose the other double-down, push on 17 and win with the 19. Basically, I will win the amount I expected to win in the first place – my original wager. At least that is what I thought would happen.

Instead the dealer revealed a 7 as her hole-card and then drew another 7!

"Are you fucking kidding me!", the dealer's words not mine! I was thinking maybe I should start side counting sevens.

If this happens to you and you lose the count because you got upset, you are going to have to walk away from the chance to get your money back. The count is still high. You better know exactly how high and you better bet accordingly or you have no business being in the casino in the first place.

You ran a computer simulation before you left for the casino and that computer played 500 million hands of Blackjack. Very likely this same scenario or maybe something more astounding happened. Do you think the computer stopped the program and decided to update Windows again? Maybe do an impromptu virus scan to clear its head?

What did your friend, DarkStar do? I made another large bet and said with a smile, "Let me see you do that again."

Easier said than done? You bet! But it's easier if you have the proper bankroll and a few months of living expenses to boot. Truth be told, at the time I had neither but pressed on anyway.

When is a Bet an Expense

You need to understand the difference between an expense and a bet. It is not as simple as it sounds. Sometimes a bet could actually be an expense or at least part of the bet. I've already explained that camouflage is an expense. So if you make a mathematically incorrect bet or play in order to avoid looking like a card-counter, then that bet was partially an expense. You might think that if the bet wins, it's a bet, and if it loses, it's an expense. The reality is, that winning or losing has nothing to do with it.

Let's look at an example to make it more clear. You know that you should hit your 16 against the dealer's 10 when the count is even or less. Since you'll be making small bets at a count of even or less, it makes sense to always stand on 16 vs 10. You'll draw less heat from casino personnel as well as other players who think you should play consistently. Of course, you should not play consistently but we already covered that.

So, what did that wrong play cost you? Sometimes you'll win anyway and sometimes you'll lose. The difference between how many times on average you'll win because you did that and how many times you'll lose, multiplied by the amount of your bet, equals the cost-of-error for that bet. The cost-of-error is the part that is an expense. In this case, the cost is a very low, .006 per dollar wagered for the average six deck game.. So, if your minimum bet is $15, you spend $0.09 every time you use this camouflage.

How you account for that in your business is up to you. For me, the cost is low enough that I ignore it. Hope my accountants Candace B. Rittenoff and Count De Monet aren't reading this. If they are, try this: Use the practice software I recommended earlier, CVBJ by QFIT and make this error every time it occurs. The software will keep track of the cost of this error for you. After you play 100 rounds, you'll have a pretty good idea how much this is costing you. Then, you just have to figure out how many rounds you play in the casino. The average 6 deck shoe with 75% penetration will yield about 15 rounds and take about 15 minutes for the average dealer. Aghhh, screw it! Let's just say it costs $5 a trip even though I'm sure it's much less.

I really just want you to understand the concept of the-cost-of-errors and how they are part of your expenses. You are going to predict results and make business plans based on what computer simulations predict. The simulations do not account for mistakes or intentional mis-plays. If you have both CVCX and CVBJ, you can actually run a simulation with some camouflage parameters. Things like No Raise After a Push, and No Large Increases in Bets, or No Increase After a Loss, can be setup in CVBJ and then imported to CVCX. Again, if you don't want to invest in the software or take the time to learn it and use it, you can submit all of this to me at www.darkstarBlackjack.com and I'll run the simulation for you.

Positive Expenses

Just like the count, expenses can have a positive or negative sign. The most obvious example of this is when you play a slot machine or some other game as camouflage and actually win. Occasionally, you may feel like you are getting heat but are not ready to leave the casino. To cool them off, you might play a little craps or slots. This can be effective at convincing surveillance that you are not a serious card counter. That is definitely an expense and winning or losing has nothing to do with it. Either way, log it as an expense but reverse the sign. So, if you spent $400 on airfare, $200 on a room and had a $300 slot win, your expenses are $300 (400 + 200 − 300). Don't overdo it on the slots or craps, etc. Remember, the only game where the player can have a legal advantage is Blackjack.

Building the Business

In the chapter on Bankroll, I talked about the possibility of a dry spell where you lose or do not win for a few months. While you do have the advantage over the house, you are still gambling. The casino is gambling too. In fact, publicly traded casinos have reported quarterly losses at Blackjack. It is very rare and I have never heard of this happening two quarters in a row, but if the house can lose over a three month period, you better believe you can too. You absolutely cannot take money from your bankroll to pay your living expenses. You would be embezzling from your own company. In addition to having other resources for living expenses, such as credit or savings, you should be building up your bankroll to withstand significant losses.

In the best case scenario, you start out winning. If you take your winnings from your first trip and buy a new car without adding some of the profit back into the bankroll, you are setting yourself up for disaster. You need to add some of that profit back into the bankroll. How much is up to you. My personal recommendation is 10 – 25% depending on the size of your bankroll and how much you need to live on. If you continue winning, you may be able to adjust your betting schedule to produce more profit without increasing risk due to the larger bankroll.

Of course, you could also start out losing. You should have a plan for that as well. If the losses are minor, you can stick to the plan. Anytime you have a loss that is greater than 2 standard deviations from the average gain, you need to find out why. Did you make mistakes? Did you use too much camouflage? Were you drinking on the job? If the loss is within normal limits but you had several in a row such that you have depleted your bankroll by 20% or more, you'll need to make some adjustments. You will need to recalculate your ROR (risk-of-ruin) using the new bankroll amount. If you have Blackjack simulation software like CVCX, you can do this very easily. You now have a choice. You can either accept the greater risk, or scale down your betting strategy to reach the same ROR as before.

Accurate Record Keeping

Just like any other business, you need to keep accurate records of all wins, losses, and expenses. I don't mean every hand, but you'll want to keep a daily total at least. You might have more than one entry for each day if you visit multiple casinos. You do this for several reasons. Obviously, you need to know if you are making money. You cannot rely on your memory for this. Not even if it is just supplemental income. Also, if this is a major part of your income, the IRS will expect you to have accurate and detailed records.

These are important reasons but may not be the most important. For me, the most important reason to keep accurate records is to improve my game. I not only keep track of wins and losses, but exactly the conditions I encounter and any important things that transpire. That way, I know which casinos have the most favorable games and what to watch out for when I return.

Also, if I have a loss that seems unusually high, I can try to figure out why. First, did it just seem high? Given the actual conditions I found, was it more than 2 standard deviations from the mean? If it was, maybe I made mistakes. I will try to relive the trip in my head. What happened that may have caused me to make mistakes? Maybe I did it on purpose because I felt I was being watched and was afraid of being barred from a good game? I made a spreadsheet that keeps a running total of my net as well as gross profits or losses. After every trip, I enter in the information. I take breaks while playing and write down what was happening either in a notebook or my phone. I do this away from the camera in the restroom or my hotel room, of course. Make sure you do this often enough that you don't forget. My spreadsheet looks something like this:

Total Expenses	Gross Profit	Net Profit						

Date	Profit	Standard Dev.	Casino	Strategy	Expense Des.	Expense Amt.	Dealer Tips	Notes

The top three are running totals, of course, and the bottom columns are where your running totals go. Under "Strategy," I keep a record of the bet spread I used, as well as the counting system and even how much camouflage I used. You can decide what works best for you. The important thing is that you are keeping these records and not relying on your memory.

Come up with a system that will allow you to keep track of exactly how much you start and end with, and make sure you find a way to keep expenses as well as tips separate from gambling wins and losses. I carry two wallets. Technically, a wallet and a money clip. Be as accurate as possible.

Employees

Personally, I would prefer not to have any employees. I included the chapter on team play for those of you who have a six figure bankroll and might need to reduce heat from the casino. If you have less than six figures for playing Blackjack I cannot see a reason for employees.

If you must have employees, then you must treat them as such. You will need to decide how you will pay them. If you are going to pay them in cash, that is fine, but you will need to file a 1099 with the IRS and give them a copy as well. You will also want to set up an LLC or corporation to protect yourself. Paying them a salary and offering benefits goes beyond the scope of this book. Even if you go the route of paying in cash and treating them as contractors, I would recommend having an attorney on retainer and probably hire an accountant as well. Now you see why I say it's not worth it unless you have a bankroll that is well into the six figures.

I strongly encourage you to perform a thorough background check on any employee or partner that you work with. Even if you don't entrust them with money, you will be trusting them with secrets about your business. They need to understand that what you are doing is legal and not cheating. You also want to make sure they understand that cheating the casino will not be tolerated. You are running a legitimate business not a gang. Stealing in any way from the casino, the business, or anyone else, will result in immediate termination and possible criminal charges. Everyone should understand that if they will be playing Blackjack as part of their role in the business, they will be playing according to the rules. Card counting is not cheating. Capping your bet (adding to your bet after you see your cards) is cheating. So is swapping a card in your hand with one up your sleeve. It is not possible to list all of the possible forms of cheating, but most of you will recognize cheating when you see it.

Taxes

Yes, you have to pay tax on gambling winnings. Also, losses can only be deducted from winnings. This is one reason to keep detailed accounting of all wins and losses on a per trip basis. You don't have to keep a record of what happened at every table unless the casino makes you fill out a form for a transaction that puts you over the $10,000 limit. You can also deduct your expenses. Make sure you keep accurate records of all your expenses. I recommend using credit cards for airfare, gas and even hotel stays in case you get audited. You are going to have to use the Other Income category for your income. This might make the IRS curious, so an audit is not unlikely. Be prepared and have good records.

I am not an accountant and I am not aware of all of the tax laws, especially since they change constantly. I have only personally paid state income tax in two states. So I have very little knowledge of your local tax laws. If Blackjack becomes your primary source of income or even a significant portion of it, you will definitely want a CPA to do your taxes and I would contact one as soon as you start seeing significant profits.

May the count be with you!

♦ Chapter 11 - Other Venues

I tell very few people that I play Blackjack for a living. When I do tell someone, the most common response is, "online?" My initial reaction was that you cannot play profitably online. This is because the cards are shuffled after every round. Counting is rendered completely useless but there actually is a way to make money playing Blackjack online. There are also tournaments, private games, smart phone apps and other places to play Blackjack. Some of these can be beaten and some may not be worth the effort even if they are beatable.

Online Casinos

I have to warn you that it is illegal in most U.S. states to gamble online with some exceptions. Also, make sure you know who you are doing business with. I have had trouble getting paid by some online casinos. Just because someone has a slick looking website does not mean they are a reputable company that will pay you when you win. You might see the credits in your account but can you actually get a check or money back on the credit card you used?

If you've done your research and believe you can trust the website, you might be able to make a little money. Many of them offer a bonus for your first deposit. You are going to have to read the rules very carefully and make sure you deposit enough money and play enough to qualify. Card-counting is not going to help you but the rules are often very favorable. Late surrender, dealer stands on all 17's, Re-split Aces, and so on. This means that the house edge may be as low as .25%.

These promotions change all of the time and I am not endorsing any of the online casinos right now because I am not positive any of them are completely honest. Say the casino is offering 200% of your first deposit up to $500 as a bonus. Make sure you understand exactly what they mean by that. In this case it says you must meet a 40x rollover of all bonus and regular chip wagers in order to withdraw them. Also, you can only play on some Blackjack games. So you will be playing a game with a .75% house advantage.

The math looks like this. You will deposit $250 to get $250 in regular chips and $500 bonus chips. For every $750 wagered you will lose $5.63. (750 x .0075 house edge = 5.63). The 40x rollover means you will have to do this 40 times. So 40 x 5.63 = 225 dollars lost to the casino. You can now withdraw what you have left. This would be $750 less $225 or $525. Subtracting your investment of $250 you have a net profit of $275. This assumes you will play Basic Strategy and lose at the average rate. Of course your actual results will vary. It is very possible that you will run out of money before ever qualifying for the 40 times rollover. It is also possible that you will profit by more than $275. You'll give yourself the best chance of hitting the average by making as small a wager as possible and keeping track of when you reach the 40 times rollover. This might be a lot of hands of Blackjack. $750 x 40 is $30,000 in wagers. If the minimum is $10 and you want to give yourself the best odds of hitting the average net profit, you would flat bet $10 3,000 times. If you are really good and have a fast internet connection. you might be able to play four hands a minute. At that rate it would take 12 and half hours to hit your goal and you will have earned about $22 an hour.

That was a real promotion offered at an online casino. I have no idea if it is still being offered and I refuse to give the name of the website because I did not take advantage of the offer and cannot confirm that they will actually honor it.

Virtual World Gaming

Blackjack can be played in the virtual world as well. In this version of online Blackjack, you create an avatar and move through a 3D virtual world. In most cases you will play with "in world currency". You can obtain this currency in a number of ways depending on the virtual world you are playing in. You can purchase the virtual currency through the creators of the world or third party exchanges. Some virtual worlds accept Bitcoin as currency.

All of the same warnings apply. It may or may not be legal. Additionally, you will want to do some research and decide if you can trust the venue. Keep in mind that many virtual worlds allow individual users to set up businesses including casinos inside the virtual world. That means you will be trusting the owner of the casino not the creator of the virtual world itself.

Similar to online, you will have to be creative to make money. In some cases you may be able to earn or be granted this "in world currency". Play using that and then exchange it for US dollars or Bitcoin. In that case you are risking nothing but your valuable time.

Smart Phone Apps

I have yet to find a smart phone app with a Blackjack game you can play for money. There are plenty of Blackjack apps that you can use to practice. Some will let you practice card counting and Basic Strategy. DarkStar Blackjack currently has one in development.

Private Games

Just like online gambling, this is very likely illegal where you live. I am not advising anyone break local laws. That said, let's say, for the sake of argument, that you already play poker with a group of friends. In many of these games the dealer is rotated and the dealer can choose which game to play. When it is your turn to deal, ask if they would like to play Blackjack. You would play as the dealer would in a typical casino and they can play however they wish. It will be single deck of course. You can let them double any first 2 cards but only allow them to split Aces once and no double-after-split. Most importantly, you will always hit a soft 17. Don't allow them all of the best player options because you might end up with a game slightly in their favor. Unlike poker, tell them, you'll deal 2 rounds before shuffling just to make sure you don't run out of cards. If it is a big poker party you might not be able to get through 2 rounds. Use your best judgment.

I did this with a group of friends one time and was amazed by how eager they all were to take me up on it. Many thought they would have the advantage since I was constrained in how to play my hand while they could hit, split or double down as they pleased. Even when I told them that, as the dealer, I would have a slight advantage, most still felt they were taking advantage of me.

The real fun comes when they decide to turn the tables on you when it is their turn to deal. They may not know you can count cards. If they give you 2 rounds like you offered them, you can use the count to adjust your bet and play. Also, they might not care how many times you split or if you double after a split. Maybe they'll even want to stand on soft 17 as the dealer. All of this favors the player but you'll pretend to just go along with it to keep it a friendly game.

Tournament Play

Tournament Blackjack is another way a professional player can make money. In a tournament, you are not playing against the house. You are competing against the other players. Card counting will help but it is not the most important skill. I highly recommend Stanford Wong's book, "Casino Tournament Strategy". Originally published in 1992, it remains the best tournament strategy book I can find.

Playing in a tournament is going to sound tempting as you improve your Blackjack skills. You are going to think that beating the average player should be easy. It is not as easy as it looks. You will want to select the right tournament conditions and understand all of the rules. You will be playing with chips that have no value and how you manage those chips will be more important than how you play your hand. I could write an entire book on playing in Blackjack tournaments but Stanford Wong already did and I don't believe I can add much.

Summary

Be careful when choosing these other venues. Undoubtedly you can think of some I may not have mentioned. I didn't think it wise, for example, to explore the possibility of playing in a mobster's basement. Blackjack is the most popular casino game in the world and you will find it in various forms in some of the most unexpected places. Blackjack is beatable but not all Blackjack games are beatable. I recommend doing your best to insure you are only risking money, not your life or liberty.

Good Luck!

Appendix - Gambling Addiction and Responsible Gaming

I think this may be one of the most important sections in the book because, Blackjack, like Poker, Slot Machines, Sports Betting, Horse Racing, Dog Racing, Roulette, Craps, Bingo, Keno, scratch cards, and all of the games you will find that people can wager on, come with the responsibility that you stay in control and don't take it too far. Just like alcohol consumption, if you have a couple of incidents that cause you or others near you to wonder, it's time to stop and self-evaluate as objectively as you can.

Having spent thousands of hours in casinos, I can recognize a problem gambler when I see one. In my opinion, most problem gamblers are actually addicted to losing. I met one gentleman who told me he had been coming to this casino almost every day for ten years and never left financially ahead. Not once in ten years did he walk out of the casino with more money than he came in with. Having played Blackjack at his table many times, I found this hard to believe. He was a better than average player and came out ahead on his share of shoes.

I said, "Surely you have been up at many different times and you just didn't bother to leave."

"That's right," he said. "I was ahead by a few hundred earlier tonight, but gave it all back, and then some."

I told him, "You need a new hobby. Maybe you should start a car collection. That way, if you get down on your luck, you could always sell a car-or-two to pay the rent."

"Maybe you're right, or maybe it's just this casino," he said.

It definitely was not that casino. The difference between a compulsive gambler and a professional player, be it Poker, Blackjack or Horse Racing, is in the way they measure success.

The addict measures success in terms of how long he/she was able to play on a given bankroll.

The professional measures it exactly opposite to that. The professional looks to make as much money as possible in the shortest amount of time.

So you can tell the difference simply by how they describe a successful trip.

The addict will say something like, "Great Night! I played for 12 hours on just 500 bucks!"

Whereas the professional would say, "That was a rough day. Took me 12 hours to make a lousy 500 bucks."

Certainly not everyone who makes the former statement is a gambling addict. They might just mean that they had a lot of fun and only spent $500. My point is that if you are measuring your success in terms of how long you can play without running out of money rather than how quickly you can reach your profit goal, you may want to step back and take an objective look at yourself.

If you think you may have a gambling addiction, this is not the right line of work for you. You have to play like a machine and cannot let your emotions make the decisions. Play with your head not your heart. Playing with heart might be OK for football, but in this sport it's brains not brawn that make champions.

A compulsive gambler should no more become a professional Blackjack Player than an alcoholic should become a wine taster.

Gambling seldom becomes a problem on your first outing or very first bet. Typically, a gambling problem progresses over time. Many people spend years enjoying social gambling without any problems. But more time consumed gambling or outside stresses can turn casual gambling into something much more serious.

Compulsive Gambling

Compulsive gambling, pathological gambling, gambling disorder are names for gambling addiction, which is a type of impulse control disorder where individuals are unable to control the impulse to gamble, despite the fact that it may be ruining their lives as well as the lives of their friends and loved ones. Gambling addiction can be present even though the individual may not be totally consumed.

Problem gambling is any gambling behavior that disrupts your life. Similar to drugs or alcohol, gambling can stimulate the brain's reward system, leading to addiction. If you're preoccupied with gambling, spending ever more and more time engaged in gambling, you are spending more and more money on it, you find yourself chasing losses, you deplete your savings, you accumulate debt, you are gambling despite serious consequences, or even resort to theft or fraud to support your addiction, you have a gambling problem.

Signs and symptoms of compulsive (pathologic) gambling include:

- Gaining a thrill from taking big gambling risks

- Taking increasingly bigger gambling risks

- Preoccupation with gambling

- Reliving past gambling experiences

- Gambling as a way to escape problems or feelings of helplessness, guilt or depression

- Taking time away from work or away from family life to gamble

- Concealing or lying about gambling

- Feeling guilt or remorse after gambling

- Borrowing money or stealing to gamble

- Have trouble controlling your gambling

- Failed efforts to cut back on gambling

- Gamble even when you don't have the money—take money earmarked for bills, children, credit cards, etc.

- You are taking out loans or racking up credit card debt to cover and continue gambling

- Family and friends have expressed concern about your gambling

- You become increasingly defensive about gambling.

Unpleasant feelings such as stress, depression, loneliness, fear, and anxiety can trigger compulsive gambling or make it worse. After a stressful day at work, after an argument with your spouse or coworker, or to avoid more time spent on your own, an evening at the track or playing the slot machines at the casino can seem like a fun, exciting way to unwind and socialize. But there are healthier and far less expensive ways to keep unpleasant feelings in check. These may include exercising, meditating, spending time with friends, taking up new hobbies, or exploring relaxation techniques.

For many people, an important aspect of quitting gambling is to find alternate ways to handle these difficult feelings without gambling. Even when gambling is no longer a part of your life, the painful and unpleasant feelings that may have prompted you to gamble in the past will still remain. So, it's worth spending some time thinking about the different ways you intend to deal with stressful situations and the daily irritations that would normally trigger you to start gambling.

Compulsive gambling is a serious condition that can destroy lives. Although treating compulsive gambling can be challenging, many compulsive gamblers have found help through professional treatment.

Most treatment for a gambling addiction resembles treatment for alcohol addiction. Treatment plans may involve a combination of counseling, medication, self-help, and support groups. If a substance or alcohol addiction is co-occurring, this addiction may need to be addressed first.

HOPE—Help and Support for Problem Gambling

If you, or a friend, or loved one might be suffering from a gambling disorder, please consider seeking professional help by consulting the resources listed below.

We recommend taking the 20-Questions form on the Gambler's Anonymous website:

(http://www.gamblersanonymous.org/ga/content/20-questions)

Help Groups

Gamblers Anonymous

T (626) 960-3500

ISOMAIN@GAMBLERSANONYMOUS.ORG

National Council on Problem Gambling Helpline

1-800-522-4700. (NCPG)

http://www.ncpgambling.org/

GamblingTherapy

www.gamblingtherapy.org

Australia

Gambling Help Online

24/7 helpline, 1800 858 858

http://www.gamblinghelponline.org.au/

Canada

Canada Safety Council--Gambling Addiction

https://canadasafetycouncil.org/community-safety/gambling-addiction

New Zealand

Gambling Helpline New Zealand

Talk to telephone counsellors for free any time on 0800 654 655, night

or day, or you can text at 8006.

U.K.

Gambleaware.co.uk

freephone 0808 8020 133

GamCare

+44 (0) 808 802 0133

www.gamcare.org.uk

Glossary

This is no ordinary glossary. I highly recommend everyone at least browse this section. You will learn about the great players of this game and pioneers of our craft.

We'd like to thank 3 major online sources that we used to put this glossary together. Without their fantastic information, this would not have been possible. Blackjackscience.com, Blackjackchamp.com, and Wikepedia.com. We encourage you to visit their websites for even more great information.

Action

A general gambling term that refers to the total amount of money wagered within a specific period of time.

[1] Amount of money bet or "put into action" by a player during entire playing session. Ten bets of ten dollars each is $100 of action

[2] Large amount of checks or cash being bet, "I've been dealing to action all night."

Ace Adjustment

Usually refers to a side count of aces kept in addition to the main count. An ace adjustment is commonly used to vary strategy and bets based upon both the main count and the number of aces counted.

Ace Neutral Count

Any counting system which does not assign a value to aces.

Ace Poor

A point where less aces than normal expectation would dictate have been dealt. The deck, pack or shoe is then considered to be ace poor.

Ace Reckoned Count

Any counting system which includes aces as a part of the main count. For example, hi-lo is an ace reckoned count, but Hi-Opt I is not.

Ace Rich

Whenever there are more aces in the deck, pack or shoe than normal expectation would dictate.

Ace Side Count

An additional count of the Aces that have been played.

Advanced Omega Ii System

A Level 2 card counting system described in Bryce Carlson's book, Blackjack for Blood. It is a balanced count which assigns the values of plus one to 2s, 3s and 7s, plus two to 4s, 5s and 6s, minus one to 9s and minus two to ten valued cards.

Advantage

Player's or more rarely the casino's expected rate of win or loss, usually given as a percentage of total money put into action. A player may be said to have a 1% advantage in a certain game. This means that the player can expect to have a 1% return on all of the money bet in that game.

Advantage Player

A player that is generally considered a professional as he is not likely to play games that he does not have the advantage.

Anchor / Anchorman

The player closest to the dealer's right which is to receive the last card before the dealer. "I'll be the anchorman or play third base". If you are new to Blackjack you may want to avoid this position. Other players will sometimes blame the anchorman for giving the dealer an advantage by not hitting or standing in the same way they would. If you're card counting, this is widely considered the best place to sit because you will be able to see more cards before making a decision on your hand.

Back Counting

Typically standing behind a Blackjack while the game is in progress and counting cards. The purpose is to enter the game only when the count is Hi or in the player's favor. This is also known as Wonging in, named after Blackjack guru Stanford Wong. The technique is particularly useful with multiple-deck shoes.

Balanced Count

Any counting system which has an exact balance between plus cards and minus cards. A card counting system is balanced when the sum of the card point values for the whole deck is equal to 0. An unbalanced count is when the sum of the point values is anything other than 0. Balanced counts include Hi-Low, Halves, Zen etc. Unbalanced counts include Red 7, K-O and Uston's Unbalanced Zen count.

Baldwin, Roger

(See Four Horsemen of Aberdeen)

One of the "Four Horsemen of Aberdeen", Baldwin is credited with creating the first accurate Blackjack strategy while serving in the US Army in the mid 1950s.

Baldwin had a master's degree in mathematics from Columbia University. He first started thinking about the mathematics behind the game of Blackjack while playing with buddies in the barracks as he served as a private in the Army.

He started working out a few formulas by hand, but soon got permission to use one of the Army's calculators to keep moving forward with his work.

Bank

This usually refers to the total amount of money a team of players and/or investors has set aside for Blackjack play. It can also refer to a single player's bankroll.

Bankroll

The total available chips or money that a player or team has set aside for Blackjack play. It can be expressed as the player's overall bankroll for the total amount of play or a session bankroll, which is the amount of money a player is prepared to bet in any individual gaming session. Another expression of bankroll often used is a player's trip bankroll, which is the amount of money a player is willing to wager during a single trip to a casino or to a gambling venue. A casino is said to have an unlimited bankroll and will cover all bets within the table limits.

Bar/Barring

To exclude from play at certain tables, such as Blackjack for counting or Poker for being obnoxious or cheating. Some people are "barred" from the whole casino. Does not necessarily imply cheating or illegal activity. Not legal in Atlantic City.

Barber Pole

A bet consisting of varying colors of chips. "Barber poles are to be broken down and paid color for color." Dealers must make sure the smallest value chip is on the top to discourage "capping" of the bet.

Basic Strategy - Blackjack - a predetermined set of decisions a player should make to maximize his average gain or expectation, while he is playing a single hand against a deck(s) of cards.

Bet

The amount of chips the player wagers on a card hand, or other game or sport.

Betting Limits/Table Limits

The set minimum and/or maximum amount of chips that the player can wager on a single bet. The player cannot bet less than the minimum or more than the maximum amount posted.

Betting Correlation/BC

A term used to illustrate the efficiency of a counting system's ability to inform the player when to increase or decrease his bet. It is usually expressed as a decimal, such as 0.95. This would mean that a count with a 0.95 betting correlation is correct 95% of the time in determining the proper bet size.

Betting Efficiency/BE

Measure of how accurate a card counting system is for choosing the optimal time to raise your bets in relation to the true count. In other words, how well a card counting system can exploit the favor ability in the deck when using a fixed playing strategy. Betting efficiency is typically measured on a scale between 0.0 and 1.0, where 1.0 is best.

Betting Ratio / Betting Spread

The range of bets which one makes while playing. If a player sizes his bets between one and ten units, then his betting spread is one to 10.

Bet Sizing Increasing or decreasing the sizes of your bets depending on whether the True Count is positive or negative.

Big Player/BP

Someone who plays in conjunction with a team of counters. A counter at a table keeps track of the count and secretly signals the big player when the count is high enough for the big player to enter the game and make a large bet or series of bets. The Big Player is signaled to come to a table by a subordinate member of the team who has been placing minimum bets and counting down the deck. When the count is very positive, the Big Player or "BP" will come to the table and place maximum bets until the deck returns to a neutral of negative condition.

Biometrica Casino Information Database Module

Developed and marketed by Biometrica Systems, Inc, the Casino Information Database (CID) module gives casinos access to an extensive database of active professional advantage players, slot and table game cheats (along with known associates), state exclusion lists, gaming scams and cheating devices. The CID database is instantly searchable by a variety of criteria increasing the efficiency of identifying casino undesirables. Biometrica actively collects information from multiple sources and provides daily database updates via the Internet to quickly distribute the most recently collected information and intelligence.

It is the software choice for casino surveillance, security, compliance and operations. The product is now utilized by over 200 casinos and gaming agencies to prevent   losses and maximize profit. Biometrica is the only software provider that provides game protection and incident reporting in one easy to use application.

Black Chip

A $100 chip.

Blackjack A hand dealt to a player that results in an Ace combined with a ten valued card.

Bet Spread The ratio between the smallest and largest bets placed by a player during one shoe. If a player's early bets are $10 , and he increases to $100 when he feels the odds are more in his favor, the he is said to be using a 10-1 bet spread.

Braun, Julian

A former IBM employee with advanced degrees in mathematics and physics, it was his advanced understanding of strategy and systems that led him to introduce major improvements in computing Blackjack strategies that would forever change the game. He contributed to significant books, such as Lawrence Revere's, 'Playing Blackjack as a Business.' In Edward Thorp's first edition of 'Beat the dealer,' the original calculations and strategies remained unclear and imprecise. It was Julian Braun's input, published in the second edition and every addition after that perfected the all important details.

At the time it was an epic feat of computer calculations using Thorp's original FORTRAN program on an IBM 707-409. After this he went on to co-develop the HI-Opt I and II counting systems with Lance Humble in the 1970's. This was a major breakthrough because it was the first accurate system that could be easily understood by a majority of players without requiring advanced degrees or heavy computation. He authored his own book in 1980, 'How to Play Winning Blackjack.'

Julian Braun died on September 4, 2000, at the age of 71.

Buck

A $100.00 wager or $100 chip.

Burn Card

A card taken off the deck - at the beginning of a new deck or shoe after it has been shuffled and before you start dealing or when a new dealer comes on duty or in the middle of a hand if a card comes out of the shoe by mistake- which the dealer slides across the table from his/her left on the right and puts into the discard rack face down or sometimes merely placed under the deck face up. This card is discarded "burned". The card may or may not be shown face up (which can affect the count if you are counting cards). It is procedure to burn a card when you are relieved to go on break. In hand-held games it is never shown. In multi-deck games it may be shown on request at some casinos.

Bust

Having a total over 21, resulting in an automatic loss.

Bust Card

The individual card that brings the hand's total over 21. **Also** The bust cards are 2, 3, 4, 5, and 6 and usually refer to the dealer's up card. If the dealer has to take a hit on hard totals of 12-16 there is a chance he'll go bust. Of course the odds get progressively better from the 2 to the 6 since there are progressively more cards that will bust him.

Buy-In

To give cash money to the dealer in exchange for chips.

Cap/Capping of Bets

To illegally add money / placing extra chips to a winning bet after you receive at least one card while the dealer is distracted (To cap a bet). Easy to detect with video surveillance.

Cage/Cashier's Cage

The place in a casino where players may redeem casino chips for cash, cash checks, or arrange credit. It is often referred to as, the cage, for short.

Cantey, Wilbert

(See Four Horsemen of Aberdeen)

One of the "Four Horsemen of Aberdeen", Cantey is credited with creating the first accurate Blackjack strategy while serving in the US Army in the mid 1950s. He started life wanting to be a priest, but was encouraged to leave seminary because of his pool hustling and card playing habits. He went on to pursue a career in mathematics, but soon after school he ended up in the Army. There, he met Roger Baldwin, and worked with him and a few other Army buddies to create the first true Blackjack strategy.

Card Down

An announcement to the floor person that a card has gone off the table. A dealer never reaches down to pick up a card, as that would expose their tray to stealing.

Card Weight

The value assigned to each card face in a counting system. This weight is added to the count as each new card is exposed. Weights are usually small integer values like minus one, plus one or plus two.

Cashier

A person who works in the cage who handles monetary transactions with players. It is similar to what a bank teller would do in a bank.

Casino Host

A casino employee who is responsible for dealing with casino patrons and answering queries about casino comps and other amenities. For example, if a rated player (professional) were to call a casino to make hotel reservations, he would ask to speak to a casino host in order to get a casino rate or a room comp.

Casino Manager

The person who manages all phases of the casino operations.

Casino Verite

A software Blackjack program designed by Norm Wattenberger that allows a person to simulate the play of Blackjack on a computer at high speed, thus enabling one to obtain the results of millions or even billions of hands of play.

Chang, John "Johnny"

(See MIT Blackjack Team)

John Chang was an MIT undergrad who joined the team in late 1980 and became MIT team co-manager in the mid-1980s and 1990s According to Wikipedia, "[Chang] reported that, in addition to classic card counting and Blackjack team techniques, at various times the group used advanced shuffle and ace tracking techniques. While the MIT team's card counting techniques can give players an overall edge of about 2 percent, some of the MIT team's methods have been established as gaining players an overall edge of about 4 percent. In his interview, Chang reported that the MIT team had difficulty attaining such edges in actual play, and their overall results had been best with straight card counting.

After having taken an elective course in the mathematics of Blackjack in 1979 he was recruited to be one of the first members of the MIT Blackjack team.

But it was at the 2005 Blackjack ball that Johnny Chang managed to really wow the elite of the Blackjack world all over again by counting down (looking at a deck that has had a few cards removed and identifying the missing cards) two decks in only 33 seconds.

Check Down/Money Down

An expression used by a dealer to inform the floor person that a chip has fallen on the floor, a situation, which requires his immediate attention.

Checks Play

A term often used by dealers to notify the pit boss that a player has made a significantly large bet. The amount of a bet that will trigger such a response varies wildly from casino to casino. It could be a bet as small as five red chips ($25) in some casinos or a bet with several black chips in other casinos.

Chips

These are tokens that the Casino uses, in place of cash, to represent a certain monetary value for making bets. You buy chips at the table. You cash chips in at the Cashier's Cage. Chips may be bought in various denominations, $2, $5, etc. Players exchange cash for chips at the tables and then cash-in their chips at the cashier's cage. Also "Checks".

C.I.D. (CASINO INFORMATION DATABASE)

Developed by Biometrica Systems, Inc, the Casino Information Databases (C.I.D.) provides casinos access to an extensive searchable database of known casino advantage players, cheats and other potential risks to their operation. C.I.D. utilizes a multitude of databases to include, law enforcement, FBI, US Marshals and Involuntary Exclusion lists by state and updated frequently.\

Cold

Term used to describe a losing cycle of hands.

Color

Each denomination of chip has a distinctive color. The standard colors are: $1 -> blue or white; $5 -> red; $25 ->green; $100 -> black.

Color for Color

The proper pay-out procedure for a dealer to pay a stack of multi-colored chips. It is faster, has less chance of a mistake, and is easier to verify by the floor person or eye-in-the-sky.

Color Up

To exchange many smaller denomination chips for a few large denomination chips. This is done as a player is preparing to leave and he may have too many chips to handle easily. "May I color up those reds for green before you leave, sir?" Then, inform the floor man. "Color up, red for green." (It also allows the floor man to see how well or poorly the player did financially.)

Comp/Complimentary

"Comps" refers to complimentary services and goods that are offered by the casino, a complimentary gift given by a casino to encourage and reward play. Comps can range from the most common, free drinks while playing, to meals, rooms, trips to resort locations and tickets to the Super Bowl.

Composition Dependent Strategy

Similar to basic strategy, but the proper play is based upon the exact cards dealt to the player rather than just the total of the player's hand. It is most commonly used for single deck games. One example of a composition dependent strategy would be doubling down on a player's hand of 5,3 or 4,4 versus a dealer's 5 or 6 in a single deck game but not doubling on a 6,2, even though all three of the player's hands would total 8.

Count/The Count

The count is the running total that is being tracked by a card counter that helps him gauge the likely value of the remaining cards to be dealt.

Cover

The use of various camouflage techniques to disguise the act of counting. It could include anything from the use of the wrong playing strategy or apparently improper bet sizing to very sophisticated maneuvers designed to fool casino personnel who may be attempting to discover whether or not a player is counting cards. Used by counters to disguise the fact that they are counters from casino personnel, such as "cover bet" and "cover plays".

Cover Bet/Cover Play

This is a bet meant to act as camouflage and mislead the dealer or floor person into believing that the player is not a card counter and the bet/s or play runs counter to the player's true strategy.

Credit Line

An amount of credit established for a player at a given casino. A player with a credit line can take a marker for any amount of money up to the amount established in his credit line and use it to purchase chips at the tables. The player is normally expected to repay the marker before the end of his visit to that casino. A credit line can be established in advance of a casino visit in much the same fashion that a loan from a bank would be obtained.

CSM (Continuous Shuffling Machine)

 A machine that mixes used cards back into the pack continuously instead of keeping them aside round after round to be shuffled all at once.

CTR (Currency Transaction Report)

A report required to be complete for cash transactions in excess of $10,000. Intended to identify money laundering for illegal activities.

Cut

To divide a deck into two parts after the dealer shuffles the cards. Generally, this is done by a player. The dealer then takes the two parts and reverses them, front to back. In most casinos, the cut is made by inserting a plastic card known as the cut card into the deck or the pack.

Cut Card

A solid colored card typically a piece of plastic which is given to a player by the dealer for the purpose of cutting the deck(s) after a shuffle and then is used by the dealer to mark the last hand to be dealt from the deck by placing it near the end of the deck in the shoe. When it comes out of the shoe, the dealer announces, "Last hand out of this shoe."

Cutoff/Cutoff Cards

This is the point at which the dealer stops dealing cards remaining in the shoe or deck.

Dealer The person at the table who represents the house or casino and shuffles and deals the cards, determines the outcome of the game and settles all wagers.

D'alembert

A betting progression system. It is a system where the bettor raises the bet one unit after each loss and lowers the bet one unit after each win. A series of numbers equidistant from one another is established, such as 1, 2, 3, 4. The player starts out by betting 1 unit. If he wins, he continues to bet one unit. If he loses, he cancels out the 1 and moves to the 2 and adds one unit to the last number, now having a series of 2, 3, 4, 5. At any point in the series where the player wins his bet, he reduces his bet by one unit. If he wins enough bets to return to a one unit bet, he starts over. If he loses during the series, he cancels out the last number he played and adds another number to the series. This system has many variations. It has never been proven to win, and in fact, cannot win in any game with a negative expectation.

Deal

The distribution of the cards to the players during the play of the game from the dealer.

Dealer

An employee of the casino who handles the gambling apparatus, cards, dice, tiles, roulette wheel, etc., makes the payoffs, and enforces the house rules at his table.

Depth-Charging

A method of play described by Arnold Snyder in his book "Black Belt in Blackjack", in which a player would either make flat bets or bet the table minimum on the first round of play after a shuffle and then raise his bets regardless of the count as play continues until the next shuffle. It is dependent upon the player seeing as many cards as possible, counting them using a counting system and making strategy variations based upon the count. In order to be successful, this method of play requires a count with a high playing efficiency and a deeply dealt single deck game.

Desirability Index

A term coined by Don Schlesinger in his book Blackjack Attack. It is a number derived by dividing the win rate by the standard deviation for the particular game being examined and multiplying the result by 100. The lowest desirability index numbers given in Schlesinger's book is -0.52 and the highest is 16.04. The higher the number, the better the game. In general terms, a player would look for a desirability index of 6.6 or higher to find game which would be considered to be playable to most counters.

Deuce

An expression used for a card numbered two (2)

Deviation

In the context of Blackjack card counting, it refers to a True Count number at which the player will deviate from basic strategy. Also known as "index".

Discard Holder/Discard Rack/Discard Pile/Discard Tray

A plastic holder to the right of the dealer attached firmly to the table. It is used to store the discards until they are ready to be re-shuffled. Red plastic is commonly used so that any marks on the cards will be amplified enough to be noticed by the floor man.

Discards

The cards which have already been played since the last shuffle. They are placed by the dealer in a discard tray on the left side of the table from the player's perspective.

Double after Split (DAS)

Casino rules that allow doubling down after the players has split any pair.

Double Deck

A form of 21 where two decks are shuffled together and dealt out of the hand. The forms of 21 are: single deck, double deck, and four, six, or eight deck shoe.

Double Down / Doubling Down

To double the size of one's initial bet before taking one more card. Once a player doubles down, the player may receive only one more card. Usually, but not always, a player may only double down after receiving the first two cards. Occasionally, a casino may allow players to double down after receiving three or more cards. Normally, the player places a bet equal to the size of the original bet next to the original bet in the betting square to let the dealer know he wishes to double down. He does this by placing an amount which may be less than, or equal to (but may not exceed) the original stake, behind his initial bet. In some casinos the player may double down after splitting and in some casinos the player may only double on 10 or 11. The Blackjack chart tells you when this is a good idea. For example, if you have a hard 10 and the dealer's up card is a bust card, let's say a 5, you would want to double down. You have a good chance of drawing an 8, 9, or 10, which is a hard hand for the dealer to beat. And there's an equally good chance that the dealer will go bust. If the dealer gets a "Blackjack", only the original bet will lose. If the player is playing in a game where the cards are held by the players, he places his cards face up in front of the betting square and the dealer places a third card either face-down under the player's bet or face up on the player's existing cards, usually at an angle opposite to the cards already in play.

Double Exposure 21

A Blackjack game in which both dealer cards are shown to the player (before) he plays his hand. Other house rules are usually changed, such as players losing pushes, and Blackjacks are paid even money to restore the advantage the house loses by exposing the dealer's hole card.

Double Up

To double down with less than 2X the original bet. Generally, when doubling is allowed, the player does not have to actually double his bet, but may increase it by any amount up to (but not more than) the original bet.

Doubling For Less

Placing an additional bet that is less than one's original wager and receiving only one additional card. Dealers must inform the floor man and receive confirmation

Down Card

A card that has been dealt face-down on the Blackjack table.

Downtown

The area of Las Vegas which begins north of Sahara Blvd. and continues to Stewart Avenue on the north. It is bounded by Main Street to the west and Maryland Parkway to the east. Some of the casinos considered to be downtown would include the Stratosphere, the Golden Nugget, the Horseshoe, the Lady Luck, Main Street Station, and the El Cortez, to name a few.

Drop Box

A box affixed to a playing table to store the money and markers exchanged at the table for chips.

Even Money

When the dealer shows an ace and the player has a Blackjack, the player can opt for even money and is paid immediately at 1:1. This is just a version of insurance, not a different bet. If the dealer has Blackjack, the hand is a push, but the player receives two times the value of the insurance, which is the same as the original bet. If the dealer does not have Blackjack, the player wins 1.5 times the value of the original bet but loses the value of the insurance, and still ends up with the value of the original bet.

Early Surrender

Player may give up or surrender after receiving first two cards but before dealer checks for an Ace in the hole. If surrendered, only 50% of bet is lost, instead of entire sum. Excellent method for controlling player losses and therefore not allowed in most casinos.

Echo

A response from the floor person when the dealer makes an announcement. When the dealer hears an "echo" the floor person is aware of the transaction and has given his approval. It keeps the dealer from turning around to look for the floor person and exposing the dealer tray unnecessarily.

Edge/House Advantage/House Edge

The ratio of the expected player loss to the initial amount bet. For example if the house edge for Blackjack is 0.5% then for every $100 you bet initially you can expect to lose 50 cents. The house edge is a good measure of expected player wins or losses over time but is not a perfect measure of comparing one game to another. The reason is the house edge does not include additional money bet (for example doubling in Blackjack or raising in Three Card Poker) as money bet. Two common mistakes in calculating the house edge are not including ties (they should be counted towards money bet) and including additional money bet (like doubling and raising) towards money bet. An exception to the usual definition is in craps, in particular proposition bets that can take multiple rolls to resolve. For place, buy, lay, and hard way bets the house edge is defined as the expected player loss per bet resolved. Another exception is in Let it Ride, in which the house edge is the ratio of the expected loss to a single bet (or 1/3 of the total initial bet).

End Play

A style of playing Blackjack in which the player takes advantage of his knowledge of the last un-played cards at the end of the deck. Happens when the player, through an increase in number of hands at the right moment and/or card-eating, manages to force the dealer to run out of cards and deal the rest of the round (or start anew) from there-shuffled discards, whose composition is favorable to the player. Extremely rare now, it was mostly practiced by self-educated advantage players in the pre-Thorp days, when single deck games were often dealt very deeply, if not completely. Nearly all casinos try to avoid the possibility of end play by cutting off some of the cards at the end of the deck or the shoe.

European no-Hole-Card Rule

A rule used in Blackjack where the dealer does not take a hole card. The dealer hand gets a second card only after all player hands are finished. If the dealer gets a Blackjack, a player who has doubled down or has split loses not only his original bet but all additional bets. The name of this rule is derived from the fact that many games in Europe and abroad are played with this rule in effect. It is not the norm in most American and Canadian casinos.

Eye in the Sky

Surveillance cameras located above Blackjack tables that allow casino security personnel to follow game play and watch players, table bystanders and dealers.

Expectation/Expected Win

A reference to what a player or the house can statistically expect to win or lose on a given bet or game. For example, the house expectation on a pass line bet at craps is 1.4%. This simply means that the house can expect to win 1.4% of all the money bet on the pass line over the long run. Since the only outcomes are win one unit or lose one unit, a 1.4% expectation means winning 50.7% of the time and losing 49.3% of the time. If the same bet were described for the player, it may be stated by saying the player on average gets 98.6% of his money back on the pass line bet (getting 100% back would be breaking even) or it could be stated that the player has a 1.4% negative expectation on that bet.

Fab Four

A term coined by Don Schlesinger used to describe the top four surrender plays that vary from basic strategy based upon the hi-lo counting system.

Face Card

The face cards are the Jacks, Queens, and Kings. They all have a value of 10. So including the face cards there are sixteen 10-value cards per deck.

Face Down (Game)

Dealing Style. In face down game, player's first card is up, second card is down. There is Face up game as well. Each style has slightly different table etiquette of play.

Face Up (Game)

Dealing Style. In face up game, both cards are dealt up and cards are not touched by player - presumably to prevent cheating. Each style has slightly different table etiquette of play.

Fibonacci/Fibonacci Sequence

Any series of numbers in which the two preceding numbers totaled together equals the next number in the series. An example would be 1, 2,

3, 5, 8, 13, 21, 34, 55. There are a number of betting progressions which utilize a Fibonacci series.

First Base

This is the first player to receive cards when the dealer deals the cards. This is the player's seat farthest to the right at a Blackjack table, from the player's viewpoint.

First Baseman

Term used to describe the player sitting closest to the shoe, on the Dealer's left hand side, and receiving the first card dealt.

Flat Betting

To wager the same amount of money on each bet made during a playing session or a portion of the playing session.

Floating Advantage

The concept whereby, in multi-deck games, the advantage we associate with every level of a True Count (TC) floats down the TC, the deeper getting into the pack of cards dealt, i.e. the deeper into the shoe the respective TC is encountered. The FA is of more theoretical than practical importance, because as a pack is depleted, the same True Count garners extra advantage, said advantage becoming especially interesting at those levels where the shuffle is most likely to occur.

Flooring

A practice which reduces every "precise" index number to just an integer (Floored indices, or indexes). When Flooring, all the index numbers are taken down ("floored") to the nearest smaller integer. Examples: +2.95 becomes +2, +1.05 becomes +1, +0.10 becomes 0, -0.05 becomes -1, -3.99 becomes -4. Notice that flooring positive numbers is identical to truncating them. Of course, an index number which has been calculated to be "precisely" an integer does not change: +3.000000 remains as +3. See also: Rounding,Truncating.

Floorman/Floor Manager

A casino executive who supervises a portion of a pit, usually under the direction of a pit boss.

Four Horsemen of Aberdeen

Roger Baldwin, Wilbert Cantey, Herbert Maisel, and James McDermott, collectively known in Blackjack circles as The Four Horsemen of Aberdeen, invented basic strategy using no more advanced tools than desk calculators and their own mathematical prowess, even before Edward Thorpe appeared on the scene with "Beat the Dealer."

The story of the four Horsemen began in 1953, when U.S. Army private and mathematics MA Roger Baldwin approached Sergeant Cantey requesting the use of the desk calculators to calculate the odds for Blackjack. He was lucky. Not only did Cantey have an interest in gambling, he also had a great passion for numbers and could not resist the lure of mathematical challenges. They soon sought the help of two other interested math buffs, McDermott and Maisel. Together they spent every spare hour of the next year and a half poring over their calculators and calculations until late in the night.

Finally they had perfected their strategy, which was radically different from the wild theories on Blackjack odds that were available at the time in that they were actually sound. In fact, when Thorp ran their numbers through the MIT computers he used for his research, they came out stunningly accurate: to a couple of hundredths of a percentage point. In 1956 they published their results in the Journal of the American Statistical Association in an article titled "The Optimum Strategy in Blackjack". A year later they published a 92 page book, now long out of print, titled Playing Blackjack to Win: A New Strategy for the Game of 21.

They never went on to win big in casinos using their own strategy, however. Maisel explains how their research turned them from that pursuit. "We were going to be rich young people ... We worked out the best way to play the game. Unfortunately, we figured out we would lose in the long run." So the horsemen never pursued the millions later teams would hunt for, though they did continue to get together throughout the years to talk about the old days.

And that, to the four Horsemen, seemed to conclude their big moment in the Blackjack world. However, McDermott, when browsing the internet, kept seeing their names come up in articles related to Blackjack. He was surprised and amused to find that without knowing it he and his friends were being honored in Blackjack circles with the nickname The Four Horsemen of Aberdeen. He contacted Arnold Snyder, whom he found most knowledgeable on the details of their story and Blackjack history as a whole. Snyder was surprised to hear from the Horsemen themselves. According to McDermott Snyder's initial response was "My God, you guys are still alive?" Snyder immediately proposed putting them forward to be included in the Blackjack Hall of Fame. All reacted with enthusiasm, and in 2008 The Four Horsemen were officially inducted. Wilbert Cantey died shortly after, on May 21, 2008.

Francesco, Al

Known as the ultimate gentleman player, Al Francesco is the creator of the very concept of team play, an idea that changed the entire history of Blackjack.

The mastermind behind the concept of the Big Player (BP), Francesco first rose to notoriety through Ken Uston's book, 'The Big Player' in 1977. Uston credits Francesco with teaching him how to count cards, and the techniques that lead Al and his various teams to extract millions of dollars. Most major players and teams over the years have employed his techniques and many are still in use today.

Al Francesco's (aka Frank Schipani, Frank Salerno) began his career as a professional gambler in his hometown of Gary, Indiana, playing Greek

Rummy and other games. He had a fantastic start, winning almost every game he played and won his starting bankroll of $5,000 in the first year, not fantastic fortune, but enough to get him started.

Al moved to California in 1963, where he read Ed Thorp's book "Beat the Dealer". He tried Thorp's Ten Count system for the first time unsuccessfully, receiving a major headache and left casino after only 20 minutes of play. But that didn't stop him from using this difficult system, and eventually, after further studies, he mastered Thorp's system and could really beat any dealer. Casinos caught up to him and after 5 years he was banned from almost every casino in the state, and had to take a break from Blackjack for long 8 years.

Francesco didn't stop learning, and having read Lawrence Revere's "Advanced Point Count system" he returned to Blackjack scene. After a short period of only a month, he started getting barred by the casinos again and stopped playing. All this made him think about a better way Blackjack systems can be utilized.

In 1971, Al started playing with teams of seven: six counters and one Big Player. He went on to recruit the team members, taught them basic strategy and "Advanced Point Count system". Once this was done, six counters were sitting at different tables, counting cards and betting small. If the count became hot, counter would make a signal to the Big Player, who would appear at a table and make big bets until the count turned again. Naturally Big Player had to appear somebody random, who just had a lucky day. Al's team made a fortune over a few years, counting cards.

One of the Blackjack players recruited and trained by Al Francesco was Ken Uston. Ken went on to reveal the team secrets to the whole world in his book "The Big Player" in 1977. This brought an end to Francesco's team. Naturally many team members hated Uston after this, but Francesco never held a grudge against him.

The array of successful Blackjack teams came to being afterwards. The MIT team, the Greeks, The Hyland team, The Czech team. They all utilized

Francesco's concept to carry out attacks in disguise and many modern teams still use the same method.

Francesco is equally revered for his amazing creativity as well as his quiet charm. He is still active in various gambling endeavors continuing to push boundaries and open up new ways of getting ahead.

GCB

The acronym for Gaming Control Board, the Nevada agency that regulates the state's casinos.

Griffin, Peter

The grandson of mathematician Frank Loxley Griffin, Peter is the iconic math genius who figured out mathematical shortcuts that would allow Blackjack players to figure out probable outcomes without requiring complex calculations.

A certifiable prodigy with a total fixation for the game, he initially proposed a course on the mathematics of Blackjack and during a session of 'research' he lost quite badly and became hooked studying games in Atlantic City, Reno and Las Vegas. He was busy determining the Betting Correlation (BC) and Player Efficiency (PE), two concepts flexible and solid enough to still be in use today.

He also accurately described the process for using single, multiple and multi-parameter counting methods without massive computer calculations.

Over 20 years he has authored several academic works and presentations on the mathematics of gambling as well as two books, "The Theory of Blackjack: The Complete Card Counter's Guide to the Game of '21'" and "Extra Stuff: Gambling Ramblings." He was the first to determine the percentage disadvantage of an "average" Blackjack player of 2%.

Peter Griffin passed away in 1998 at the age of 61.

Grind

1. To make money in small increments while gambling.

2. To eke out a profit over the long run.

Grosjean, James

The youngest member of the Hall of Fame, James Grosjean got his start like a lot of other Blackjack masters at the mathematics department of a major university in his case Chicago University. As the story goes his interest was sparked when he noticed a sloppy dealer hole card and began calculating strategies

That was the beginning. Since then he has contributed a wide variety of well explained and comprehensive player tactics, such as card counting, for Blackjack as well as many other casino games that had not received the level of in-depth attention that Blackjack has. These included: Caribbean stud poker, Big Six Wheel, Craps, Let It Ride and Three Card Poker. These can be found in his influential book, 'Beyond Counting: Exploiting Casino Games from Blackjack to Video Poker,' released in 2000.

Grosjean is best known for his legal battles that contributed to the demise of the Griffin Agency, the much hated group responsible for compiling player databases of suspected cheats, card counters or anyone the casinos didn't particularly like. For over 10 years the agency had assisted casinos all over the world in banning and harassing players. But on September 13, 2005 it was over. The Griffin agency was forced to file for bankruptcy after James Grosjean and Michael Russo were successfully awarded $45,659 in damages due to their mistreatment as a result of information given to the casinos by the Griffin agency.

Perhaps even more impressively he continued his legal battles with Caesar's Palace, the Imperial Palace and two Nevada Gaming Control board agents. After being pushed around, threatened and wrongfully held by security at the Imperial Palace and a local jail, he was awarded $599,999 in 2005.

H17

An abbreviation used to signify that the rules of a particular Blackjack game include requiring the dealer to hit a soft seventeen.

Hand

1. The cards held by a player or the dealer to form a complete play.

2. A reference to a completed round of play.

3. A completed play at other table games, such as craps.

Hands per Hour

An estimate of the number of Blackjack hands played per hour in various conditions.

Hard Hand

Hands without an ace or with an ace valued at 1 are said to be hard in that they can only be given one value, as opposed to "soft" hands. Any hand that does not contain an ace presently being counted as 11. Or to put another way, a hand in which there is a chance the player will bust on a hit.

Hard Total

The total of any hand not containing Aces or the total of a hand where the Ace is counted as 1. So a 10 and an 8 is a hard total of 18, or a hard 18. An Ace and a 7 is a hard total of 8.

Heat

The pressure a casino puts on a winning player, typically someone who is suspected of being a card counter. It can range from very mild forms, such as a pit boss intently watching a player, unnecessary comments to more overt forms, such as a pit boss counting down the cards in the discard tray, particularly after a player has raised his bet, accusations of counting cards, intent scrutiny of your game by the pit bosses or other casino personnel. Most counters consider heat to be a warning sign that the casino suspects they are counting.

Hi-Lo Count

A balanced level one counting system which values the 2 through 6 cards as a plus one and the tens, face cards and aces as a minus one. It has become the universal language of card counters, in the sense that many of the standard references to the count in games use the Hi-Lo count as a basis, such as the Illustrious 18. Often, when there is no other frame of reference, if someone refers to a count number, it is assumed that the reference is based on the Hi-Lo count. The most comprehensive guide to the Hi-Lo count can be found in Stanford Wong's book, Professional Blackjack.

Hi-Opt I

A balanced level one counting system included in Humble and Cooper's book, The World's Greatest Blackjack Book. It assigns the value of plus one to 3's, 4's, 5's and 6's and minus one to ten valued cards.

Hi-Opt II

A balanced level two counting system which is sold separately from the Hi-Opt I system. It assigns a value of plus one to 2's, 3's, 5's and 6's, plus two to 4's and 5's, and minus two to ten valued cards.

High Roller

A person who makes large wagers in the casino. What constitutes a high roller in one casino may be very different from one casino to another one. For example, a $100 bettor may be considered a high roller in a small downtown casino such as Fitzgerald's, but wouldn't attract too much attention at the Mirage.

High-Low Light

Card counting system similar to Red Seven, but slightly more powerful. Recommended for those having mastered Red Seven.

Hit

To ask for another card. If that extra card makes the total over 21, then the player busts.

Hole Card

The second card to be dealt to the dealer that is dealt face down and not revealed to players until after they have acted upon their hands.

Hyland, Tommy

Manager of the longest running Blackjack team in history, Tommy Highland is highly respected for his success at the tables as well as his straightforward and polite manner. Where all other professional Blackjack teams have broken up for all kinds of reasons ranging from jealousy and greed to anxiety over losing streaks, Tommy has inspired and lead his team since 1979.

The original group started with just $4,000 contributed by each member but quickly made more than ten times that. Because Tommy has been around since the very beginning of the Atlantic City casinos his team has seen all kinds of action from concealed computers (when legal), Big Player techniques, card counting, shuffle tracking and ace sequencing.

While Tommy has played by and merely tested the rules at casinos, it hasn't always been a friendly career. When Atlantic City cracked down on many of the loopholes that made Blackjack a prime target in the late 1970's, his original team all left to take advantage of greener pastures in Asia. Tommy stayed behind and rebuilt the team with friends he had made through golfing, another game of concentration and skill.

Even after all these years of playing within the law things can still get sketchy. He's been harassed and threatened, arrested and worse. In 1994 the Hyland team was arrested in Ontario, Canada for an Ace Sequencing scheme. Tommy chose to fight back and legally beat the casino again when the judge ruled that such strategies were not illegal or cheating but the use of intelligent strategy thanks to the expert testimony of fellow player Arnold Snyder.

Illustrious 18

A term coined by Don Schlesinger to describe the 18 most advantageous deviations from basic strategy, based on the Hi-Lo count. The 18 plays described equal about 80% of the gain that could be had from playing the full set of indexes in more complex strategy tables.

Index Number

A term often used by counters to identify the count for specific strategy deviations. For example, the proper index number for standing on a hard 16 versus a dealer's 10 is 0, using the Hi-Lo count.

Insurance

If the dealer's up card is an ace (or ten as up card), he or she will call for insurance. When you place an insurance wager, you are betting that the dealer has Blackjack. To make an insurance wager, pace an amount, up to one half your original bet on the insurance line when the dealer calls for insurance. If the dealer has Blackjack you win your insurance bet, but lose your original bet. If the dealer does not have Blackjack, you lose your insurance bet and the game continues. Taking the insurance bet is highly advantageous to the house, unless the player is card counting.

Junket

An organized group of gamblers that travel to a casino together. Junkets are usually subsidized by a casino to attract players.

Kaplan, Bill

(See MIT Blackjack Team)

Bill Kaplan, a 1980 Harvard MBA graduate who had run a successful Blackjack team in Las Vegas three years earlier. Kaplan had earned his BA at Harvard in 1977 and delayed his admission to Harvard Business School for a year, when he moved to Las Vegas and formed a team of Blackjack players using his own research and statistical analysis of the game. Using funds he received on graduation as Harvard's outstanding scholar-athlete, Kaplan generated more than a 35 fold rate of return in less than nine months of play. Kaplan brought discipline to the team insisting it had to be run as a business with formal management procedures, a required counting and betting system, strict training and player approval processes, and careful tracking of all casino play.

For a while, Kaplan dropped out of the card counting game, only to partner up with Massar again in the early 90's to form Strategic Investments. Now the MIT Blackjack Team was more profitable than ever, and it's now 80 members generated millions of dollars in revenue. In 1993, Strategic Investments paid out its final dividends and dissolved.

Labouchere

A betting progression, also known as the cancellation system. A bettor chooses a series of two or more numbers which add up to the profit he intends to make. He then bets the total of the two outside numbers in the series and cancels those numbers if he wins. He continues betting the two outside un-cancelled numbers until he has completed the series. If he loses a bet, he adds the amount of his loss to his series as a single number. He must therefore cancel out two numbers for each number added. This system is a good way to lose good money fast.

Las Vegas Strip/The Strip

The portion of Las Vegas Boulevard which extends roughly from Sunset Road to Sahara Boulevard. It includes many of the most well known casinos in Las Vegas, such as the Mirage, Caesar's Palace, the Flamingo Hilton, New York - New York, Circus Circus and the Bellagio, to name a few.

Late Surrender

 A Blackjack rule which allows the player to forfeit half of his bet after seeing the dealer's up card, unless the dealer has a Blackjack, in which case the player loses his entire bet.

Law of Large Numbers

 In probability theory, the law of large numbers (LLN) is a theorem that describes the result of performing the same experiment a large number of times. According to the law, the average of the results obtained from a large number of trials should be close to the expected value, and will tend to become closer as more trials are performed.

Ma, Jeffrey

(See MIT Blackjack Team)

Jeff Ma or Jeffrey Ma was a member of the MIT Blackjack Team in the mid-1990s. He graduated from Phillips Exeter Academy. He attended MIT where he graduated with a degree in mechanical engineering in 1994. He was the basis for the main character of the book Bringing Down the House (where he was renamed Kevin Lewis) and the film 21 (where he was renamed Ben Campbell). Ma also co-founded PROTRADE (a sports stock market website, that has since been shut down) and does consulting work for professional sports teams including the Portland Trail Blazers and San Francisco 49ers. He cofounded Citizen Sports, a sport-information website and iPhone application based in San Francisco, which was acquired by Yahoo! in May 2010.

His first book, "The House Advantage: Playing the Odds to Win Big In Business" was published in July 2010 by Palgrave Macmillan. Ma is a regular speaker at corporate events and conferences where he talks about how to use data and analytics to make better business decisions.

Ma makes a cameo in 21 as a Blackjack dealer named Jeffery at the Planet Hollywood Resort and Casino. Jim Sturgess's character, Ben Campbell, refers to Jeffrey as, "my brother from another mother."

Ma is currently the CEO and Founder of tenXer, a San Francisco based startup, with the vision to "...make work better and your work better".

Ma joined ESPN in November 2014 as their Predictive Analytics Expert. Per this arrangement, he does weekly TV appearances on SportsCenter and contributes as a writer on ESPN.com.

Maisel, Herbert

(See: Four Horsemen of Aberdeen)

Marker

An IOU to the casino signed by a player who has casino credit.

Martingale

1. One of the oldest betting progressions in existence. It requires a player to double the size of his bet after a loss and to continue doubling his bets until a win is achieved, resulting in a profit equal to the size of the original bet. It is impossible to win in the long run using this system.

2. As a Blackjack system, the martingale system is not very useful. The whole idea of the system and this seems intuitively simple is, using basic Blackjack strategy, to double your bet every time you lose. If you lose again after that, you double your bet once again, and so on. The idea behind this is that you'll have to win eventually, and when you do, you'll get all of your money back, plus a little more.

This may sound all fine and good, until you consider the fact that there's a table limit. This means that if you start out with a $2 bet, for instance, that can quickly double to $4, $8, $16, $32, $64, $128, $264, and suddenly you've hit the table limit. Any money you made before on your small $2 wins is lost if you get up this far and lose. And the odds are, you will lose eventually. On the last bet of this betting series, you'll have put down

$518, all in an attempt to make 2 measly bucks.

The truth is, all systems are destined to lose. Trying to win with Blackjack systems can be compared to trying to get a positive number by adding negative numbers together. Nope, the only Blackjack system that will help you is card counting, and that's why we are here.

3. Often used as a term for any system which requires increasing a bet after a loss. It is not a winning method of betting in any form.

Massar, J.P./a.k.a. "Mr. M"

(See MIT Blackjack Team)

In May 1980, J. P. Massar, known as "Mr. M", according to a History Channel documentary, overheard a conversation about professional Blackjack at a Chinese restaurant in Cambridge. He introduced himself to the speaker, Bill Kaplan, a 1980 Harvard MBA graduate who had run a successful Blackjack team in Las Vegas three years earlier. Kaplan had earned his BA at Harvard in 1977 and delayed his admission to Harvard Business School for a year, when he moved to Las Vegas and formed a team of Blackjack players using his own research and statistical analysis of the game. Using funds he received on graduation as Harvard's outstanding scholar-athlete, Kaplan generated more than a 35 fold rate of return in less than nine months of play

Massar wasn't nearly as successful as Kaplan at card counting, and was in fact wondering if the MBA graduate would help him out. Luck was in Massar's favor because Kaplan had just parted with his former Blackjack team, and was looking for a local group to play with.

After going to Atlantic City to watch Massar and the other MIT students play, he saw numerous card counting errors such as using different systems, making betting mistakes, arguing over irrelevant math formulas and putting little time in at the Blackjack tables. Based on his observations, Bill Kaplan told Massar and his friends what they were doing wrong, and agreed to train them if they followed his rules and training schedule.

Mezrich, Ben

Born in Boston, Massachusetts, Mezrich is best known for his first non-fiction work, Bringing Down the House: The Inside Story of Six MIT Students Who Took Vegas for Millions (ISBN 0-7432-4999-2). This book tells the story of a group of students from MIT who bet on Blackjack games using a sophisticated card counting system, earning millions of dollars at casinos in Las Vegas and other gambling centers in the United States and the Caribbean. The story was made into the movie 21, released in 2008. Despite being categorized as non-fiction many of the characters in Bringing Down the House are composite characters and some of the events described have been contested by the people the characters are based on.

A variety of stories about a few of the players from the MIT Blackjack Team formed the basis of The New York Times best-selling Bringing Down the House, written by Ben Mezrich. While originally marketed as nonfiction, Mezrich later admitted characters and stories in the book were mostly fictive and composites of players and stories he had heard about through hearsay. The private investigation firm referred to as Plymouth in Bringing Down the House was Griffin Investigations.

Mezrich wrote a follow-up book, Busting Vegas, which took even greater liberty with the actual happenings of the team. Many events in this book were at least partly based on incidents that occurred during the team's Strategic Investments era.

MIT Blackjack Team

Mezrich graduated magna-cum-laude with a degree in Social Studies from Harvard University in 1991 and is the author of several other books.

MIT Blackjack Team

The MIT Blackjack Team was a group of students and ex-students from the Massachusetts Institute of Technology, Harvard Business School, Harvard University, and other leading colleges who used card counting techniques and more sophisticated strategies to beat casinos at Blackjack worldwide.

The team and its successors operated successfully from 1979 through the beginning of the 21st century. Many other Blackjack teams have been formed around the world with the goal of beating the casinos.

The MIT Blackjack Team continued to play throughout the 1980s, growing to as many as 35 players in 1984 with a capitalization of as much as $350,000. Having played and run successful teams since 1977, Kaplan reached a point in late 1984 where he could not show his face in any casino without being followed by the casino personnel in search of his team members. As a consequence he decided to fall back on his growing real estate investment and development company, his "day job" since 1980, and stopped managing the team. He continued for another year or so as an occasional player and investor in the team, now being run by Massar, Chang and Bill Rubin, a player who joined the team in 1984.

The team played on and off the next few years but interest waned as casino conditions, player exhaustion, and weakened management focus caused the group to lose players and finally stop playing.

The MIT Blackjack Team ran at least 22 partnerships in the time period from late 1979 through 1989. At least 70 people played on the team in some capacity (either as counters, Big Players, or in various supporting roles) over that time span. Every partnership was profitable during this time period, after paying all expenses as well as the players' and managers' share of the winnings, with returns to investors ranging from 4%/year to over 300%/year.

In 1992, Bill Kaplan, J.P. Massar, and John Chang decided to capitalize on the opening of Foxwoods Casino in nearby Connecticut, where they planned to train new players. Acting as the General Partner, they formed a Massachusetts Limited Partnership in June 1992 called Strategic Investments to bankroll the new team. Structured similar to the numerous real estate development limited partnerships that Kaplan had formed, the limited partnership raised a million dollars, significantly more money than any of their previous teams, with a method based on Edward Thorp's high low system. It involved three players: a big player, a controller, and a spotter. The spotter checked when the deck went positive with card counting, the controller would bet small constantly, wasting money, and verifying the spotter's count. Once the controller found a positive, he would signal to the big player. He would make a massive bet, and win big. Coincident with this new funding, the three general partners ramped up their recruitment and training efforts to capitalize on the opportunity.

Over the next two years, the MIT Team grew to nearly 80 players, including groups and players located in Cambridge, New York, New Jersey, Pennsylvania, California, Illinois, and Washington. Sarah McCord, who joined the team in 1983 as an MIT student and later moved to California, was added as a partner soon after SI was formed and became responsible for training and recruitment of West Coast players.

At various times, there were nearly 30 players playing simultaneously at different casinos around the world, including Native American casinos throughout the country, Las Vegas, Atlantic City, Canada, and island locations. Never before had casinos throughout the world seen such an organized and scientific onslaught directed at the game. While the profits rolled in, so did the "heat" from the casinos, and many MIT Team members were identified and barred. These members were replaced by fresh players from MIT, Harvard, and other colleges and companies, and play continued. Eventually, investigators hired by casinos realized that many of those they had banned had addresses in or near Cambridge, and the connection to MIT and a formalized team became clear. The detectives obtained copies of recent MIT yearbooks and added photographs from it to their image database.

With its leading players banned from most casinos and other more lucrative investment opportunities opening up at the end of the recession, Strategic Investments paid out its substantial earnings to players and investors and dissolved its partnership on December 31, 1993.

Money Plays

Cried by the dealer to alert the pit boss when a player puts down money as a bet without wanting to exchange them for chips. Also said by the player to the dealer, declaring that he doesn't want the money changed into chips.

Monkey

A face card, probably a corruption of "monarchy." Shouted by players from Far East (Vietnam, Laos, etc) when asking for a good hit from dealer when doubling down.

N0 (N Zero)

The number of hands (sometimes expressed in hours of playing time) theoretically required to be played with a certain set of rules and strategy (count, spread etc.) before the player reaches his goal to be ahead by at least one standard deviation. It has been supported as a main measure of every situation's (rules & strategy) assessment mostly by Brett Harris. Some thought is achieving N0 for two standard deviations are comparable to the "long term".

It is expressed as N0 = Var / EV^2. N0 for two standard deviations if N0 * 4.

Natural

When an Ace and a 10 value card are dealt as the first two cards totaling 21 in value. This hand typically pays 3:2 odds and can also be referred to as a Blackjack.

Never Bust Strategy

To never risk hitting a stiff hand (12,13,14,15,16) in Blackjack.

No Double After Split (NDAS)

Casino rules that do not allow doubling when the player has split two cards.

No Hole Card

This describes any Blackjack game in which the dealer does not take a second card until after all player hands are finished. If a player who has doubled down or split loses only the original bet to a natural by the dealer, the player's strategy and edge are the same as if the dealer took a hole

card and checked it. If the player loses all on doubles and splits against a natural, the game is generally called "European No Hole Card".

Oscar's Grind

A conservative win progression described by Allan Wilson on pages 246-248 of The Casino Gambler's Guide. After a loss, you repeat the bet. After a win, you bet whatever you need to show a total profit of one unit, subject to increasing your bet no more than one unit. Like all progressions, Oscar's system does not change the casino's edge.

Over/Under (O/U)

Two side bets that can be made in Blackjack. In the over bet, the player is wagering that his two card total will be less than 13. In the under bet, the player is wagering that his total will be more than 13. In either case, if the total is exactly 13 the player loses. Aces count as one in considering the card totals.

Parlay

1. This is a reference to increasing the size of one's bet by the amount won on a previous bet.

2. It refers to increasing one's overall bankroll in a session or number of sessions, such as, "He parlayed his $1000 bankroll to $4000 after two months of play."

Penetration/Deck Penetration

Used to quantify the location of the cut card in a given Blackjack game. Sometimes expressed as a percentage, "This shoe has a 75% penetration."

Also expressed as "The shoe has 1.5 decks cut off".

For Blackjack purposes, "penetration" refers to how deeply into the cards the dealer deals before shuffling. For example, if the dealer deals 5 decks before shuffling in a 6-deck game then the penetration would be 5/6 or 83%. Penetration is extremely important to card counters, the greater the penetration the greater the advantage.

Pit

The area in the casino surrounded by table games. While it is often confined to one specific type of game, it can include any of the table games. It is the area where casino personnel track the games and the players, among other duties and is where employees such as pit bosses and floor men can be found. Casino patrons are not allowed access to the pit.

Pit Boss

Casino staff member who checks and monitors all of the casino play within his/her designated pit area.

Pitch

A Blackjack game dealt from the hand of the dealer using 1 or 2 decks.

Probability

The probability of an event is the number of ways that event can occur, divided by the total number of possible events that could occur. For example, there are 4 ways to be dealt a Royal Flush in a 5-card hand (one for each suit), and there are combine (52,5) =2,598,960 possible 5-card hands that could be dealt, therefore the probability of being dealt a Royal Flush in 5 cards from a 52-card deck is 4/2598960 = 0.00000154.

Progression Betting

A form of betting which requires one to change the size of his bet based upon the results of the last hand or series of hands. Progressions can be negative, which usually means a bet is raised after a loss, or positive, which usually means the bet is raised after a win. No progression has ever been devised which can change the actual expectation in any given game.

Push/Stand Off/Tie

Same as tie. Player's hand equals dealer's, assuming neither has 21. In a normal Blackjack game, the player's bet is returned to him when a push occurs. In double exposure games and in many charity games, the player loses on a push with the dealer.

Rack

1. The special place in the table where the dealer keeps the house chips, stacked horizontally in rows. Also Tray.

2. In some casinos, players can ask for racks to hold their chips.

Rainbow Blackjack

Variation of Blackjack which identifies each player's position at the table with a color. Each player has betting spots for each of the other colors, allowing him to bet on other players' hands as well as his own. This game is not widely offered, seen mainly in southern Mississippi.

Red Seven Count

An unbalanced counting system devised by Arnold Snyder and included in his book, "Blackbelt in Blackjack," which strikes good balance between power and ease of use. It gets its name from the fact that the player counts only the red sevens as plus one and assigns a zero value to the black sevens. The other values assigned include plus one for 2's, 3's, 4's, 5's and 6's and minus one for ten valued cards and aces.

Revere, Lawrence

The father of professional Blackjack playing, and author of the first heavily influential guide to Blackjack, 'Playing Blackjack as a Business.'

Like many other members of the hall of fame, Lawrence Revere is also a unique character with a life story that sounds more like the plot of a movie than a standard author bio. Starting at the age of 13 in the back of a smoke leaden barbershop in rural Iowa he began dealing cards before leaving to study mathematics at the University of Nebraska. As soon as his degree was inked he set out west to begin playing professionally in 1943.

Lawrence Revere is one of the few Blackjack authorities famous for having been on every side of the game: working as a dealer, pit boss, owner and player for over 28 years. In the 1960's and early 1970's he was considered the preeminent Blackjack expert.

His often remembered boast was that he was 'barred from playing in all Nevada casinos.' And for good reason. He was the first to conceive, utilize and eventually publish several breakthrough counting strategies that have proven to be the foundation for Edward Thorp and Julian Braun's later work as well as countless others.

He was admitted to the hall of fame posthumously after passing away in 1977 due to lung cancer.

Rider Bet

The bet made by a player (the "Rider") behind another player's bet. Most casinos allow two Riders max. The total amount of bets placed on the betting circle (spot) cannot exceed the table maximum. In most casinos, the player who has the original bet on the spot gets to direct how the hand will be played. The original bettor also gets to fill up the spot up to the maximum bet at any time, if he so chooses, leaving out anyone else who wishes to place Rider bets. In some casinos, the player who gets to direct the play of the hand is the player who has placed the largest bet, even if he's a Rider. If a Rider has the option of making the extra bet on pair splits, there are some variations to basic strategy that can help the rider. Also "Over-the-shoulder bet".

Risk of Ruin

Describes the likelihood of losing all of one's bankroll.

Rounding

A practice which reduces every "precise" index number to just an integer (Rounded indices, or indexes). When rounding, all the index numbers are rounded to the nearest integer, following the mathematical rules which apply when rounding numbers. Examples: -1.50 becomes -2, -1.49 becomes -1, -0.50 becomes 0, +0.49 becomes 0, +0.50 becomes +1, +1.49 becomes +1, +1.50 becomes +2. Of course, an index number which has been calculated to be "precisely" an integer, does not change: +3.000000 remains as +3.

Rule of Six

A policy followed by many casinos at single deck. They require a dealer to deal five rounds to one player, four rounds to two players, three rounds to three players and two rounds to four players. Some casinos carry this rule to the extreme and only deal one round to five or more players.

Running Count

The total number of points a card-counting system assigns to the cards seen from the beginning of the deck or shoe. The running count is updated by the value of the point count after each hand.

S17

An abbreviation for the casino rule which requires the dealer to stand on all soft 17s.

Schlesinger, Donald "Don"

Don Schlesinger is a gaming mathematician, author, lecturer, player, and member of the Blackjack Hall of Fame who specializes in the casino game of Blackjack. His work in the field has spanned almost three decades. Don began his professional life teaching mathematics and French in the New York City school system. In 1984, he changed professions and, until 1998, was a principal (executive director) at a Wall Street investment bank. Since his retirement from the finance industry, he has devoted even more time to Blackjack, in a researching, writing, teaching, and playing capacity.

His contributions to the game include research into optimal betting, risk analysis, optimal back counting, Floating Advantage, camouflage and team play, and card counting systems comparison. He is best known for creating the *Illustrious 18*, an abridged set of the most efficient card counting indices mentioned in most card counting books published in the last 30 years. He also created DI (Desirability Index) and SCORE (Standard Comparison of Risk and Expectation), to optimally compare games under various scenarios. Schlesinger has edited, consulted and/or collaborated with many of the leading Blackjack analysts, programmers, and authors. He has a B.S. degree in mathematics. In addition, he holds M.A. and M.Phil. degrees in French from the City University of New York.

Sequencing

An advanced shuffle-tracking, team technique. The players identify certain cards (usually Aces, hence "Ace Sequencing") in the shuffle and by controlling the table attempt to subsequently steer these cards to the team's hands.

Session

A short period of time for recording results. A session might be the time you spent at one table, or the time you spent in one casino, or the time you spent playing Blackjack between breaks away from the game.

Settlement

The resolution of the bet. The dealer either collects the player's chips, pays the player or leaves the chips on the table in the case of a push.

Sharpe Ratio

A method of comparing risk and ruin, named after Nobel Prize winner William Sharpe. It compares the difference in return and investment may have over a risk-less investment to the risk of the original investment.

Shoe

This is the shoe box shaped transparent or wooden device that holds up to eight decks used in Blackjack. It allows the dealer to deal one card off the top quickly and efficiently. Two, four, and six deck shoes are common.

Shuffle

To thoroughly mix the cards before dealing them to the players.

Shuffle Card

A plastic card, usually the same as the cut card, which is inserted into a deck, pack or shoe to indicate when to break the deck and reshuffle the cards.

Shuffle Master

The trademarked name of a mechanical device that some casinos use to shuffle the cards in multi-deck games, in order to speed up the game and defeat cheating and shuffle tracking.

Shuffle Tracking

A sophisticated technique that requires a player to count the cards, observe where groups of high or low cards are placed in the discard tray, follow them through the shuffle, and then cut the cards in such a way as to bring excess high cards into play. It is a proven way to get an edge at shoe games.

Shuffle Up

Premature shuffling by the dealer to discourage card counting or to harass a player who is usually suspected of being a counter. Also preferential shuffle.

Side Bet

A bet in Blackjack that may be made in addition to the primary bet placed in the betting circle. It is similar to the proposition bets in craps, in that the player is betting that a certain circumstance will occur, such as receiving a pair or two cards of the same suit. Almost all side bets carry a large house advantage.

Side Count

An additional count to track certain cards. Common side counts include an ace or five count.

S.I.N. (SURVEILLANCE INFORMATION NETWORK)

Developed and marketed by Biometrica Systems, Inc., Surveillance Information Network (S.I.N.) is a real-time alert system which enables the sharing of information between all participating casinos and law enforcement agencies. By using the S.I.N. network, casinos can identify patrons, suspects and persons of interest to greatly reduce potential losses. S.I.N. offers a broad network of more than 200 casinos and gaming agencies located in the United States, Canada, Puerto Rico, Bahamas and Aruba.

Snyder, Arnold

Arnold Snyder is one of the definitive Blackjack experts on the planet and the self proclaimed "Bishop of the Church of Blackjack." His nine published black jack books, numerous articles and online resource have become landmarks for both formula and strategy as well as a commitment for exposing frauds.

Because of his intense knowledge and professional accomplishments his expert testimony at Tommy Hyland's 1994 Ontario court battle with a local casino is the main reason why team play is legal in the United States and Canada today.

He is one of the most important authors on the subject of Blackjack for good reason. Beginning with the ground breaking, 'The Blackjack Formula' he was the first to accurately describe the concept of deck penetration or depth of the deal used in card counting. His books when taken together almost read like the encyclopedia of Blackjack, from 'The Blackjack Shuffle Tracker's Cookbook,' also the first to describe his mathematical analysis for shuffle tracking in used in the large modern decks, as well as how to track the ever more complex shuffling methods the casinos had devised.

For enthusiasts interested in the fascinating history and personalities in the Blackjack world his, The Big Book of Blackjack is a great read. Arnold Snyder has also remained active in advocacy and current issues as an editor of Blackjack Forum an online resource for professional Blackjack players.

Arnold Snyder doesn't stop at dealing with math and tactics of Blackjack. He takes interest in the players behind the game too. His "The Big Book of Blackjack" provides an amazing overview on history of the game itself as well as giving insights on the landmark figures that made Blackjack so popular and influenced the game considerably.

He gives not only technical details and facts but also has a great sense of humor, thanks to which it is so interesting and exciting to read Snyder's writings.

Arnold Snyder was never in favor of various computer devices that help gamblers win, but he became a sponsor of PowerSim – the software that simulates card counting. According to him this program is helpful in learning tools, rules, good bets and strategies of Blackjack.

Soft/Soft Hand/Soft Total

A hand that contains an Ace which is counted as 11. E.g. Ace-9 is soft 20.

"Soft" denotes that the value can be changed. If later valued at 1, it becomes a "hard" hand.

Soft Double

To double down on a hand with an ace as part of the original hand.

Spanish 21

A version of Blackjack in which the actual tens are removed from play. It carries a variety of favorable rules, and can be beat with specialized counting methods.

Split/Splitting Pairs

To split a matched pair of cards in Blackjack and play each card as a separate hand. Usually, any pair of ten valued cards may be split as if they were a natural pair. You place an additional bet equal to your original bet on the separated card. In most casinos if the second card on either or both of these 'new' hands make another pair, you can split that hand as well. Some casinos do not allow Aces to be resplit. When splitting pairs, as with "Doubling Down", if the dealer gets a "Blackjack", only the original bet will lose.

Splitting Aces

If you receive a pair of aces on your first two cards, you may choose to split the aces. When you split aces, you will receive only one card on each ace. However, if you receive a second ace after you split, in some casinos you may choose to re-split the aces.

Stand / Stay

The decision not to draw any further cards, or hits. For example, a person dealt two tens would normally stand and refuse another card. The dealer will proceed to the next player.

Standard Deviation

A term which describes how far one may stray from the expected value of a game in either direction. It is determined by finding the square root of the variance of a game.

Stiff/Stiff Hand

1. Any hand that could bust if drawn to. For example a hard 12-16. The stiff hands are hard totals of 12 through 16. 2. A reference to any dealer up card of 2 through 6, since we always assume a 10-value card in the hole. "The dealer was showing a stiff."

Stop Loss

A pre-set limit to the amount of money a player is willing to lose in any given session.

Streak

A series of wins or losses. A whole sector of Blackjack-theory is devoted to the quest of identifying streaks before they occur, in violation of all natural & scientific laws.

Surrender

Surrender is the only option of not playing a hand after receiving your first two cards. When you exercise the option of surrender, the dealer will pick up your cards, and you will lose one half of your bet. This is done before the dealer plays out his hand.

Taft, Keith

Keith Taft is the undisputed gizmo genius of Blackjack. Along with his son, Marty, they have created some of the most innovative and insane gadgets for beating the casinos.

Starting when his son was still a teenager and for the last 30 years they have wired cameras, fabricated tiny computers and innumerable communications gadgets with incredible creativity. Their inventions are the highlight of the Barona Blackjack museum.

Their first computer, named George was a 15 pound large rectangular monster that dripped acidic battery acid burning Keith during the trial run. A few years later a major leap occurred with the next version: David. More than just being a pocket sized version of George it also improved the calculation method by using Thorpe's Hi-Low technique and this helped make it simple and straightforward to use.

In 1977 after winning $40,000 in one week they set up production to sell the device at $10,000 a pop. Unfortunately the winning streak came to an end quickly when the casinos caught on. Luckily when Marty was busted no one from the casinos to the FBI could figure out exactly what the device was and he was let go.

It was only in 1985 that the state of Nevada outlawed counting machines. By then shoe cameras and every other casino beating device had been successfully tested and used.

Target /Target 21/T.A.R.G.E.T.

Acronym for Table, Research, Grading and Evaluation Technique. An alternative system, originally formulated by Eddie Olsen and Jerry Patterson, to beat multi-deck Blackjack. TARGET's basic premise is that casino shuffling routines are non-random and tend to create biases in shoes, sometimes favoring the player (5% of the time) but mostly favoring the house (70%). The player must therefore identify and play in tables that show evidence of excess players' wins while avoiding tables which are "dealer-biased". A set of table-selection rules is provided, which focus on signs of players crowding the table (a lot of cigarette butts in the ashtrays, etc), for specific card sequences ("clumping") observed, etc. The system has been totally and convincingly shown to be pure snake oil, by a number of Blackjack authors, through computer simulations, statistical analysis & logical arguments. [References: See Break the Dealer 1986 and BJ: A Winner's Handbook 1990, both by J. Atterson, for the system's presentation. Also see the comprehensive Sims on biased shoes in

Blackjack Essays by Mason Malmuth, 1987. Also see Abdul Jalib's analysis of biases in his "In Search of Clumping" post archived in bjmath.com. See also Professional Blackjack by Stanford Wong 1994, for simulations and exhaustive analysis of streakiness & bias resulting from various shuffling procedures.

Third Base / Third Baseman

The seat at a Blackjack table which is the farthest to the left. It is the last person to receive the cards during a round of play. Also Anchorman.

Thorp, Edward O.

Best known as the author of the Internationally renowned book, 'Beat the Dealer' Edward Thorp was a mathematics professor at MIT who proved that Blackjack could be won through a technique referred to as Card Counting.

He completed undergraduate and graduate work at U.C.L.A., receiving the B.A. and M.A. in physics, and the Ph.D. in mathematics in 1958. He has taught at U.C.L.A., M.I.T., and New Mexico State University and was Professor of Mathematics and Finance at the University of California at Irvine.

He was among the first pioneers of computer aided devices for Blackjack even learning to program in FORTRAN on an IBM 704 with a special emphasis on card counting schemes and cards that were not reshuffled at the end of a deck.

To prove his theories this nutty professor headed off to Las Vegas with $10,000 in money fronted by mobster Manny Kimmel. He won $11,000 in the first weekend before being kicked out by security. Current shuffling rules at casinos are a direct result of Dr. Thorp's success.

Once proven he published his book which instantly jumped to the top of the New York Times Best Seller list. He is noted in academic circles for this process as being the first to eschew traditional academic publishing in order to go directly to a mass audience for his findings as well as risking very real physical damage to verify a computer simulation. He was also the first to use a computer as a gambling aid.

Beat the Dealer was not an easy read for ordinary players at first, because it was difficult for average gambler to use Thorp's theory in live casinos. Along came the second edition of the book in 1966. Julian Braun assisted Thorp in making this edition more down to earth, so that ordinary players could understand it and utilize it at casinos.

Thorp didn't stop at casinos, he applied his knowledge and success with "Beat the Dealer" to the ultimate casino: The Stock Market. In 1967 "Beat the Market" came out. Together with co-author J.Regan, Thorp created a system, helping to read the stock market and play it similarly to a casino game.

He went on to help people invest in the stock market via his own firm "Edward O. Thorp & Associates". Thorp made a considerable fortune in the securities market and through his own hedge fund.

Tray

The special place in the table where the dealer keeps the house chips, stacked horizontally in rows. Also rack.

True Count

The true count is derived from the running count divided by the number of decks left in the shoe. The running count adjusted to account for the number of cards left in the deck or shoe to be played. The total number of decks can be estimated to the nearest deck or half deck.

Truncating

A practice which reduces every "precise" index number to just an integer. (Truncated indices or indexes). When Truncating, we simply take away (truncate) the decimal part of the index number, leaving only the integer part. Examples: +2.95 becomes +2, +2.15 becomes +2, -0.99 becomes 0, -3.05 becomes -3. Of course, an index number which has been calculated to be "precisely" an integer does not change: +3.000000 remains as +3. Also Flooring and Rounding.

Up Card

The dealer's first dealt card, placed face up.

Uston, Ken

A Yale University and Harvard MBA graduate, Ken Uston is known as the flagrant personality of Blackjack for his wide range of controversies and contributions. For most he is known for his books, "Million Dollar Blackjack" and "The Big Player." This was a result of his association with Al Francesco, who recognized Ken's skill counting cards and made him a member of his team utilizing Al's concept of the Big Player (BP).

This idea had a team of players at various tables in the casino counting cards and when a count became extremely positive team members would flag down the designated Big Player of BP who would make a significant bet. At the time this bypassed the casinos security and was highly successful. After the book was published Al Francesco's team was barred from playing in Las Vegas and a long standing feud began.

When Atlantic City became a gambling mecca in 1978, Ken moved to New Jersey where he was quickly banned from the casinos for card counting. Just as fast he counter sued the casinos stating that skilled players could not legally be banned. In 1982 the New Jersey Supreme court ruled in his favor and card counting, at least is still permissible. However in direct response casinos have added decks and moved up shuffle points to reduce the advantage for skilled players like Ken.

To get past security at casinos where he was banned Ken Uston is equally famous for his incredible range of disguises both physical as well as with cards.

In the early 1980's when computer games came out he became fixated with Pong, Space Invaders and PacMan due to their obvious patterns. Highly creative in his attempts to 'crack' these games he authored a new book on the subject and became the inspiration for computerized Blackjack games created for the Apple II series, Atari 8-bit family, Commodore 64 and IBM PC.

Ken Uston died in 1987 at the age of 52 in Paris, France.

Uston Advanced Plus/Minus Count

A level one counting system described by Ken Uston in the book, Million Dollar Blackjack. It is a balanced count which values the 3 through 7 cards as a plus one and the tens, face cards and aces as a minus one. It also utilizes a number of strategy variations based on the count.

Uston Advanced Point Count

A level three counting system described by Ken Uston in the book, Million Dollar Blackjack. It assigns the value of plus one to 2s and 8s, plus two to 3s, 4s, 6s and 7s, plus three to 5s, minus one to 9s and minus three to 10s.

Uston Simple Plus/Minus Count

See Uston Advanced Plus / Minus Count. It uses the same tag values but does not include the strategy variations on the Advanced Count.

Variance

This can be determined by subtracting the expected value from each possible outcome in a game or hand, squaring the differences and multiplying each square by its probability of occurring and then summing the total of the product.

Vig

1. A colloquial expression for the house advantage on a game.

2. Used to describe any fee collected for play. It derives from a gangland term for the interest charged by loan sharks and is short for vigorish.

Whale

This is casino-speak for a super high-roller of the biggest sort. Casinos will do most anything to attract these players.

Wong, Stanford

A pseudonym for John Ferguson, Stanford Wong started his gambling career while pursuing a PhD in finance from Stanford University in 1970. He burst onto the Blackjack scene with his 1975 classic, 'Professional Blackjack,' which popularized a technique known as 'Wonging.'

It was the first instance of players keeping count of a game and only placing a bet after the count had become positive and then stepping out again. It proved so popular that casinos now usually bar this style of play. He also devised a cleaver method for handling the large 4 deck shoe games that has lead many professionals to refer to card counting as 'pre-Wong' or 'post-Wong.'

He then traveled extensively through Asia encountering many different kinds of Blackjack games and in his out of print, 'Blackjack in Asia,' he describes his many and highly creative strategies for beating all of them. Beyond a simple guide it also describes his adventures in illegal currency exchange and customs protocols.

In 1980 He published another breakthrough called, 'Winning Without Counting,' a collector's item that describes both legal and illegal card methods with a voracious sense of humor.

His computer program, Blackjack Analyzer was originally created for personal use but later became one of the first commercially available odds analyzing tools on the market.

He has authored over 15 books, all on Blackjack and has contributed enormously to many other important Blackjack books, publications and websites. He currently maintains his own Blackjack website that describes the rules and conditions of Blackjack tables in casinos around the world.

Wong/Wonging/Wonging-In/Back Counting

Typically involves a counter standing behind a Blackjack table while a game is in progress and counting cards. The purpose is to enter the game only when the count is Hi or in the player's favor. This is also known as Back Counting. The procedure was devised by Blackjack Guru Stanford Wong

Zen Count

A level two counting system described by Arnold Snyder in his book, "Blackbelt in Blackjack." It assigns a value of plus one to the 2s, 3s and 7s, plus two to the 4s, 5s and 6s, minus one to the Aces and minus two to the ten valued cards.